Breaking the Treasure Code

The Hunt For Israel's Oil

by

James R. Spillman

&

Steven M. Spillman

True Potential Publishing

Travelers Rest, South Carolina

Published by:
True Potential Publishing
PO Box 904
Travelers Rest, SC 29690
info@tppress.com
www.tppress.com

ISBN 978-0-9767811-9-6

Library of Congress Control Number: 2007934418

Printed in the United States of America

<u>Dedication</u>

To the memory of James R. Spillman, who walked with God and served Him in life. The evidence of his labor on earth continues today to bear fruit in the lives of those he touched.

"Being confident of this very thing, that he which hath begun a good work in you will perform it until the day of Jesus Christ:" Philippians 1:6

Acknowledgements

John Brown of Zion Oil & Gas Company for his continued faith and dedication to the fulfillment of the promise of oil in Israel.

> *Also concerning the foreigner who is not of thy people Israel, when he comes from a far country for Thy name's sake (for they will hear of Thy great name and Thy mighty hand, and of Thine outstretched arm); when he comes and prays toward this house, hear Thou in heaven Thy dwelling place, and do according to all for which the foreigner calls to Thee, in order that all the peoples of the earth may know Thy name, to fear Thee, as do Thy people Israel, and that they may know that this house which I have built is called by Thy name.*
>
> *I Kings 8: 41 – 43*

The Zion Oil & Gas Company team, for their time and instruction in their individual fields of expertise.

Jerry McGlothlin of SpecialGuests.com for his advice and brilliant title suggestion.

Theologian Dr. Roger Luther for his study and analysis of related scriptures.

Always to my wife, friend and partner, Elaine. Every venture is a joint venture.

CONTENTS

Book I

Oil! • Moses' Blessing • Between His Shoulders?
• Joseph's Head Returns • The Blessings of the
Other Brothers • "Blessings of the Deep that Lieth
Under" • Another Hebrew Parallelism • Joseph is
Represented by His Two Sons • "Rejoice in Thy
Going Out" • Gad of the Torn Arm • Asher Dips
His Foot in Oil • The Fountain of Jacob • Is
Joseph's Well an Oil Well?

Book II

Permian! • Problems in the Hole • Signs for
Above • The Bratzlav Hasidim • Developing
Ma'anit 1 • Plan B • Equipment • Moving
Forward

The Economy • Geo-Political Situation • Energy •
Problems • Stakeholders • The Israeli Perspective
• Jews and. Christians • The Christian Perspective
• The Arab Perspective • Not Enemies (sort of) •
The Boycott • The Moslem World • The
Palestinian Problem • The Palestinian Perspective
• The World's Perspective • Russia • Western
Europe • China and the Far East • The US
Perspective

Ishmael, Isaac, Jacob, & Esau • Perspective • The
Lesson • God's Purpose • Prophecy Fulfilled •
The End of Days • Gog and Magog • The End
Game

APPENDICES

INTRODUCTION

This is the second printing of _Breaking the Treasure Code; the Hunt for Israel's Oil_. This edition has been revised and updated from the original 2005 printing. In the last two years the story of Israel's oil has expanded and the political situation in the Middle East and the world at large has become more dire. As world events escalate and the promise of Israel's oil nears its fulfillment, the story behind Jacob's Blessing only becomes more relevant. This 2007 edition includes many of the events that transpired in the two years between printings. This is a living story, every year it comes closer to its conclusion.

*****

Stories of hidden treasure have fascinated people for thousands of years. The discovery of an ancient map, clues hidden in a forgotten manuscript, scattered fragments of a mysterious puzzle; all of these pieces, finally coming together, leading us to a treasure that has been hidden for ages. The clues, the map, the ancient stories; they all fit together into a single picture; a picture that reveals the nature and location of a vast treasure.

Beware though! Hidden treasure often holds a purpose of its own. Buried long, long ago, intended to be uncovered later, when the circumstances for its use were ripe. The treasure's first owner, its rightful owner, had his own purpose in mind when he buried it here.

What if the treasure is discovered today? Will it serve the purposes of those who discover it, or does it have some hidden purpose, something its original owner intended from the beginning?

Perhaps the treasure was meant to lay hidden until a time when its original purpose could be served. Perhaps now is the time. But what purpose could its first owner possibly mean for the treasure to serve today?

The Hunt Begins

This book is the story of a treasure hunt; possibly the most important treasure hunt in our history. Not just because of the size of the treasure; but because of the implications of its discovery. When this treasure comes to the surface the world will change. Its unearthing may herald the end of this age of man and the beginning of a new age.

Many steps of the treasure hunt have already been completed. The clues have been revealed. The X has been located. The hole has been dug. The treasure has been sighted.

The part of the story yet to be told is what will happen when it is brought to the surface. Will it bring blessings to those who find it? Will it bring a curse? What will the neighbors think? Whose purpose will the treasure serve? Does it have a purpose of its own; maybe that of its original owner? Discovering the treasure is one thing, what happens when it comes to the surface will be another thing entirely!

Our treasure story begins at a kitchen table in Southern California. The year is 1973. A grocer and a preacher sit at the table.[1] Spread out before them are paper cut-outs; a map of Israel, cut into puzzle pieces. They are in the shape of Israel's twelve ancient tribal territories; delineated more than three thousand years ago.

A Bible lays open, in front of the grocer. A notepad, filled with scribbled remarks is at his right hand. He explains

---

[1] Jim Gerard (the grocer) and Jim Spillman

the puzzle, excitement rising in his voice as he moves pieces into place, flipping the pages of his Bible to obscure passages in the books of Genesis and Deuteronomy.

The preacher listens, politely with just a hint skepticism; then, as the grocer unfolds his story and the map pieces come together, his interest mounts. At first the scriptures seem vague and unrelated, but together they build to make the grocer's case. Unbelievably, the map confirms the scripture clues - head, crown, foot, and arm! "This is something. This is really something!" the preacher thinks.

Finishing his explanation the grocer glances up, searching for some reaction in the preacher's eyes or in the expression on his face. The preacher shakes his head, amazed at what has just been revealed.

"Jim," he says to the grocer, "we'd better pray about this." They bow their heads over the map pieces, notes and open Bible spread out in front of them. The clues have been revealed. The treasure hunt has begun.

The Book

Jim Spillman, wrote _The Great Treasure Hunt_ in 1981. It was a small paperback; just 79 pages. It wasn't his first book, certainly not considered his most significant at the time. Pictured on its cover was a father with his two young sons, the dress and background was that of ancient Egypt. A parchment map and a Russian battle tank were behind the father and sons scene. A large red "X" was painted on the map. How these seemingly unrelated images tied together was anyone's guess.

The back cover gave the reader ominous clues about what lay inside. Three bulleted questions:

"WOULD YOU LIKE TO KNOW:"

- Where the greatest treasure in the world is buried?

3

- Why will Russia attack Israel?

- The secret behind the battle of Armageddon?

Pretty big questions for such a little book.

Jim Spillman was a teacher and a Bible scholar. He held advanced degrees in history and Greek. Biblical prophecy concerning the Apocalypse (the last days of this age of man) was a specialty and his position was often different from the popular view. His approach was original and unique and his results often reflected equally. The message conveyed in _The Great Treasure Hunt_ didn't disappoint when it came to original and unique.

Biblical prophecy describes an event in which the armies of the world, led by "Gog and Magog" would invade Israel "to take a spoil". The book's thesis was born with the question, "What could Israel possibly possess in the last days that would make it such a prize for conquest that the world's armies would meet there to fight for the spoils?"

Israel's high-tech sector is respectable and her agricultural products are world-class but she doesn't possess wealth enough to warrant the world's avaricious interest to the point of invasion. Countries don't invade their neighbors for pomegranates and olive oil ... but they do go to war over another kind of oil.

Recent history has proven that petroleum oil is worth going to war over. It is feasible that Israel's enemies would invade to "take a spoil" if she possessed vast oil reserves.

The problem, however, is that Israel is an oil poor country. Fifty years of oil exploration and production in Israel have produced about 20 million barrels total. That's a little over two days of the oil production currently coming out of Saudi Arabia. Armies will go to war over oil, but not two days worth.

But what if a significant amount of oil was discovered in Israel; a really significant amount? Fifty billion barrels … maybe more? Fifty billion barrels is a lot of oil. At $70.00 per barrel it adds up to three and a half trillion dollars.

Fifty billion barrels would satisfy Israel's current oil consumption needs for more than 500 years. With such a vast reserve Israel could become an oil exporting country. Israel, at fifty billion barrels, would rise into the world's top ten countries with greatest oil reserves.

Fifty billion barrels of reserves by itself wouldn't make Israel a target for invading armies. Venezuela has fifty-three billion barrels of reserves; and as of this writing there has been no news of armies on the march to Venezuela to plunder her oil supply. Venezuela, however, is not a small Jewish State surrounded by enemies sworn to wipe her off the face of the earth. Israel unfortunately is. The fact of her geographic location and the sentiments of her neighbors makes Israel's situation a little more interesting.

The Message

The Great Treasure Hunt was published in 1981; why republish it today, twenty-six years later? Its original message, like a seed planted in the hearts of a few believers back then has grown over the years into a tree, ready now to bear fruit. As a tree grows the seasons take their course and cast their effect on the tree's growth and the flavor of its fruit. In the seasons that have transpired since this seed was planted in 1981 world events have unfolded, preparing this message to bear fruit at its proper time.

This story is now much nearer its completion than when the first little paperback was released. The whole story didn't begin in 1981, however. Long before man's story on earth began, natural events were set in motion that would have profound implications today, even then preparing for the close of this present age. Nearly four thousand years ago a blessing was given and a promise was made by a father to his sons; a promise that his sons would "suck honey from the rock" and "oil from the flinty rock." This promise, to the sons of Jacob, the people of Israel, is on the razor's edge of its realization. This book is the herald of this promise's fulfillment; and of its profound consequences.

Construction

The annotated edition of the original manuscript, **Book I**, explores the incredible implications waiting to explode in the Middle East when this treasure is brought to the surface. From the Middle East events will spread like a wind fanned fire beyond the region to the world at large. The realization of Jacob's Blessing will not just change the tenuous geo-political balancing act in the Middle East; it will become a crucible of decision, forcing the governments of the world to choose between Israel and her enemies.

Any additions to the original manuscript in Book I will appear inside of a shaded text box. This separation will denote information not included in the original manuscript.

Book II relates the stories of those who believed the message and threw their lives and fortunes into _The Great Treasure Hunt_.

These stories are the result of more than two decades of searching for the treasure that lays buried deep beneath the sands of Israel. The collective research and discoveries of have provided scientific proof of the treasure's existence. These modern day treasure hunters have, just now, begun to tap its vast vault.

The Reason

As profound as the discovery and implications of Israel's oil will be, there is another more important reason for this story; an eternal reason.

This was not just a promise and a blessing given by Jacob to his sons. This is a promise and blessing given by God to his people. The story of oil in Israel is part of the greatest story; the story of God's plan and purpose for man.

The promise will be fulfilled. The oil will be brought to the surface. The abundance and implications of the discovery will become reality. But this will happen, not because Jim Spillman uncovered a thread of clues that reveal the treasure's location, or because faithful men have spent their lives and fortunes on its quest, or because Israel will benefit from the abundance oil will bring. This promise will be fulfilled because it is part of a greater promise. The promise that man will be reconciled with God and that this age will end and a new age will begin.

Breaking the Treasure Code

The Hunt For Israel's Oil

Book I

CHAPTER ONE

AN ETERNAL COVENANT
FOR THE ISRAEL OF GOD

The Lord promised Abraham that he would make of him "a great nation," that he would give him a land, a country that would be for his "seed." Later on God told Moses about this "promised land" and that it would be flowing with milk and honey (Exodus 3:8). Moses was then directed to lead the children of Israel out of Egypt to the Promised Land, which finally he did. God had prepared this special land. He promised it to Abraham's "seed." God always keeps his promises.

Moses encamped with the children of Israel at Paran and then sent twelve men secretly into Canaan to "search" it out. The spies returned with giant fruit and the report that indeed the land was flowing with milk and honey (Numbers 13:1–27). They also reported that there were giants in the land and that it was too dangerous to go into the land, "promised" or not. Only a small minority, two, Joshua and Caleb, gave a positive report regarding defeating the giants. Later, when the children of Israel did cross the Jordan and go into the land to possess it, God gave them strength and wisdom to defeat the giants.

God promised them rich land. He would help them "possess it," was his added assurance. Beginning with

Abraham and God's covenant with him, we see two focal points: the land and the people. God promised that he would bless and protect the people, and that he would give them the land "for an everlasting possession" flowing with "milk and honey" (Genesis 17:8 and Numbers 13:27).

> The whole land of Canaan, where you are now an alien, I will give as an everlasting possession to you and your descendants after you; and I will be their God." (Genesis 17:8 NIV)
>
> They gave Moses this account: "We went into the land to which you sent us, and it does flow with milk and honey! Here is its fruit. (Numbers 13:27 NIV)

Riches Underground

This covenant was an unconditional covenant. God said that he would do it, and true to his word of promise, he did it. The question of the land being rich on top has never been in doubt, but what of the natural resources under the ground? For most of history, agriculture was the basis of economy and livelihood. Land was valued for its surface richness. But since industry and super industry took over the world economy in the twentieth century, the riches under the surface of the land became far more valuable than the fertile soil. As I began this study my questions flowed forth:

> "Lord, you know everything. You know what is going to happen before it happens. You knew that these last days were coming. You even spoke of the 'last days' in Genesis. You also knew that oil would be the single most valued commodity during the end times. Why would you have the children of Israel wander over some of the richest oil lands of the Middle East, and direct them to settle on oil poor real estate? It would be different if the land wasn't an 'everlasting possession'. It would be understandable. But you promised in your Word 600 years before the birth of Christ that 'Israel' would return

in the 'latter days' and the land would produce even greater riches than before!"

> After many days thou shalt be visited: in the latter years thou shalt come into the land that is brought back from the sword, and is gathered out of many people, against the mountains of Israel, which have been always waste: but it is brought forth out of the nations, and they shall dwell safely all of them.
>
> (Ezekiel 38:8)

I asked another question: "Petroleum, how did you become so precious, so necessary and indispensable, when you were once nothing but grimy sludge?"

CHAPTER TWO

FROM OLIVE OIL TO PETROLEUM

Oil has been use for various purposes for thousands of years. It is not known just when man began to use vegetable oil. Different plants were used, but olive oil proved to be the most versatile and desirable. It was used as a lubricant, an illuminant, for cooking and in medicine. When the use of oil is mentioned in the Bible, it is usually olive oil that is meant.

Bitumen, petroleum seepage on the surface of the ground, has also been used since man's history began. The Greek historian Herodotus, in the fifth century B.C., describes some of its uses and even where to find it.

There isn't much more that would be helpful in our study concerning the ancient use of oil. But the ancient understanding of "what oil was" is cogent to our search. Invariably when "oil" was used it was vegetable oil, mostly olive oil. Bitumen, when it could be found, was used, but was primitive in its unrefined state, and its uses were limited. The ancient mind never understood it as *"oil."* The concept of oil springing up from the ground was beyond their imaginings.

No word for *petroleum* existed in pre-exile Israel. The Old Testament Hebrew word, "shemen" meant literally "liquid grease" or "slimy stuff"; a generic term used for any liquid vegetable or animal fat. "Zepheth," the ancient Hebrew word for bitumen (softened asphalt), as far as we know, was never related to the concept of liquid petroleum oil.

15

The years passed, by the hundreds and then the thousands. Finally, in the 1800's discovery and use of petroleum became a reality. Oil was processed from shale rock in Scotland in 1850. However, it took American ingenuity and expertise to drill the world's first oil well, on August 27, 1859, at Titusville, Pennsylvania. What a timely discovery it was too, as the United States was in the beginnings of the Industrial Revolution – a revolution that would change the world!

I wonder if the first drill-hand (roughneck) there in Titusville knew just how historic he was. This bubbling crude was to change man's welfare and his warfare. Wars could be won and countries lost because of this black grime that he was now wiping from his forehead. The future of the world was on his face!

From Titusville to Opecville

At first, petroleum was used for basic necessities such as fuel, lubricants, illuminants, and certain questionable medical purposes. By the time the new century rolled around (1900) many more uses and users were found. Hundreds of new oil wells were producing, and John D. Rockefeller, leading Standard Oil Company, was well on his way to becoming the "richest man who ever lived."

Standard, as well as others, now began to search the world for new "fields." New strikes were discovered here and there, but none as large or as lucrative as the Middle East oil fields. The first oil strike was in Persia in 1908, and by the beginning of World War II the Middle East would be recognized as the greatest area of oil production in the world. As late as 1970 it could be said that 60 percent of the known oil reserves in the world were around and under the Persian-Arabian Gulf.

According to the U.S. Energy Information Administration, as of March 2005 proven oil reserves in the Persian Gulf nations were estimated at 729.3 billion barrels; about 57% of known world oil reserves. If you add in the former Soviet states and North African nations the percentage of total known reserves jumps to over 69% of world reserves.

Intense and sophisticated research and technology entered the "oil business" by the end of World War II. More petroleum products were discovered and quickly made available to a waiting public. Fuels, lubricants and illuminants were more refined. Solvents and surfacing materials were developed. Soap, detergents, fertilizers, insecticides, synthetic rubber for tires, man made fibers for clothing, paints, plastics, medicines, and even TNT were placed under the petroleum Christmas tree.

Every year saw not only new products from petroleum, but new users of the products. More wells were drilled, but the thirst for oil was vampiric. The veins of the earth were opened wider and deeper. The jugular in the Middle East was gushing from every incision, trying to quench an insatiable thirst that by the 1970's was demanding 1,500,000,000 gallons a day! Oil had become the single most important item of international trade.

A barrel of oil equals 42 U.S. gallons. According to the Energy Information Administration, as of the first quarter of 2007, world oil demand is at 85 million barrels per day (3,570,000,000 gallons), more than twice the world demand in the 1970's.

By 1960, certain oil-exporting countries felt the need of unity and concerted decision and action. In 1960, Saudi Arabia, Iran (Persia), Iraq, and Kuwait joined Venezuela as the charter members of OPEC (The Organization of Petroleum Exporting Countries). Thirty years later there would be many more members of OPEC.

Although demand was outrageous, world supplies were still higher than world demand, and the Saudi production was so high that the market held steady at around $2.00 a barrel all through the 60's. Gasoline was the greatest American bargain. Giant automobiles would guzzle this cheap fuel at 10 times the rate of any other country. The United States, drunk for so long on cheap gas, was about to experience its first case of the D.T.'s, for a blood feud that had broken out 3,900 years ago was about to break out on its bloodiest, most costly battle yet.

Prayer, Blood and Oil

The autumn of 1973 will go down in history as the "beginning of the end." As the Arabs launched their surprise attack against a truly surprised Israel, forces were being put into motion that would change the world! Aside from the grim reports of casualties and carnage of the intense war effort on Yom Kippur, world political and economic change was also triggered. The international body politic was in seizure.

The Arabs were fighting a *total* war. One of the most important things that they could do to cripple Israel was to cut off her oil supplies and the supply of any nation that aided her. On October 17, 1973, that is exactly what happened. Arab oil producers, in a Kuwait meeting, voted to reduce the output of oil. Some of the Arab states stopped altogether the export of oil to the United States.

The following month, on November 6, the Common Market, completely dependent on the free flow of Arab oil, endorsed a document calling for the Israelis to withdraw from occupied territories.

The United States, Israel's only strong ally, found herself increasingly isolated by world opinion. The other power blocs of the world were pro-Arab. The communist bloc was supplying arms to Syria and Egypt. The Pan-Arabian power bloc and its "diplomatic" tool, OPEC were at war with Israel.

Europe had spoken through the November 6th EEC statement and couldn't afford to befriend Israel. Japan and the non-aligned industrial nations desperately needed Arab oil.

Some nations even felt that the U.S. had been the catalyst to start the Yom Kippur war. In the summer of 1973, during the debate of the Israel-Arab situation in the United Nations Security Council, the Council had been highly critical of Israel's continued occupation of Arab territory. The Council was moving toward a unanimous vote of censure, only to be stopped by the solitary veto of the United States.

The oil embargo of 1973, which produced a controlled supply of oil, signaled the end of petroleum's supply overage in the world. Demand now exceeded supply. This caused oil prices to double and then quadruple, and that was just the beginning!

"Peace" was finally negotiated. The Arabs were richer. Both sides were wiser in the ways of war. Israel had lost world influence. Arabia, acting in concert, was now a world political power. Yom Kippur had brought a change in the balance of power. The United States and the Arabs were reconciled through the efforts of Henry Kissinger, but from this moment on America would not ever again be quite as "pro-Israel" as she had been. Her heart was in Jerusalem, but her gasoline credit card was lost somewhere in the shifting sands of Arabia.

Later Oil Discoveries

1979-81 brought new petroleum discoveries. There had been new wells drilled, to be sure, but these are not the discoveries to which I am referring. These three years had seen the phenomenal rise of crude oil prices. What was "discovered" is that we can no longer easily afford to buy gasoline for our cars or fuel to heat our homes.

1979 was called the year of crisis in the oil world. Iran was the reason. The overthrow of the Shah and the subsequent political upheaval caused Iran's huge oil production to staunch and then subside almost completely. The United States was hurt severely over this, as ten percent of her oil imports came from Iran

A check on prices at this time is most revealing. The first quarter of 1979 saw *Arabian light* crude oil selling at $13.34 a barrel. When the revolutionary Iranian students took the American hostages captive on November 4, 1979, *Arabian light* went to $41.00 a barrel – *African light* went to $43.00 (In 1972 this same oil sold for $2.00 a barrel)!

> The United States has not purchased Iranian oil since 1979. Iran produces about 4 million barrels per day for world consumption. In July 2005 the "spot price" for crude oil topped $77.03 per barrel.[1]

If 1979 was the "year of crisis," 1980 was the "year of surprise." The surprise came in the strange behavior of the oil markets. Experts were not able to tell just what was going to happen or to whom it was going to happen. 1981 saw more of the 1980 surprises. The supply had (temporarily) matched demand, but the prices continued to drift up!

The money flowed rapidly from the West to the Middle East. The Morgan Bank ran several computer scenarios, and every one of them had OPEC with a surplus running into hundreds of billions of dollars, five hundred billion dollars in three years. That's the biggest amount of money ever let loose in the history of the world. All that money and all that oil!

Israel, on the other hand, apparently neither had money nor oil. She was hopelessly outnumbered, she was poor (inflation running over 100%), and she had no oil. She was

---

[1] http://tonto.eia.doe.gov/oog/info/twip/twip.asp

constantly in danger of national extermination. If only she had oil!

Hidden Riches

Is there black gold, oil, in Israel? Did God deposit secret riches in the land of promise when He "divided unto the nations their inheritance?" Is that kind of thinking within the character of God? I, for one, believe that it is. Let us read Isaiah 45:3:

> And I will give thee the treasures of darkness, and hidden riches of secret places, that thou may knowest that I, the Lord, which call thee by name, am the God of Israel.

Verse four adds that he is doing this for "Jacob my servant's sake." Are "the treasures of darkness, and hidden riches of secret places" describing great oil deposits hidden deep in the earth? They could very well be, for this Bible text is addressed to Cyrus, not to Israel! Look at the first verses of Isaiah forty-five:

> [1] Thus saith the Lord to his anointed, to Cyrus, whose right hand I have holden, to subdue nations before him; and I will loose the loins of kings, to open before him the two leaved gates; and the gates shall not be shut;
>
> [2] I will go before thee, and make the crooked places straight: I will break in pieces the gates of brass, and cut in sunder the bars of iron:
>
> [3] And I will give thee the treasures of darkness, and hidden riches of secret places, that thou may knowest that I, the Lord, which call thee by name, am the God of Israel.
>
> [4] For Jacob my servant's sake, and Israel mine elect, I have even called thee by thy name: I have summoned thee, though thou hast not known me.

21

We know that it was this very Cyrus who brought Persia into power in Babylon and then signed the decree of release for the captive Jews. Cyrus founded the Persian Empire. He was unknowingly used of God "for Jacob my servant's sake."

But what about "the treasures of darkness, and hidden riches of secret places?" Does this mean that Persia had oil under its land? That must be exactly what it means, for it was in Persia in 1908 that the first oil well in the Middle East was drilled. If God rewarded Cyrus with an oil treasure for "Jacob my servant's sake," would it not be commensurate with his character to bless Jacob in the same manner?

> The Hebrew word "neft," (equivalent to the English word "naphtha") came into existence as a result of the Israelites' Persian captivity around 500 BC. This was the first Hebrew word usage that meant specifically "petroleum oil." Apparently there is a connection between God's promise of "the treasures of darkness, and hidden riches of secret places" to Cyrus and petroleum![2]

If it is indeed within the character of God to act in this fashion, is it then to be found in the plan of God? In other words, if God would act this way, did he? The *only* place we can find an answer to that is in the Bible. But where would we start to look? Should we look up "oil" in Strong's Exhaustive Concordance and discover the first use of the word *"oil"* in the Bible and go from there? No, that wouldn't work at all, for as we have already stated, "oil" in the Bible meant either animal fat or olive oil. No Bible writer or character had the conceptual capacity to imagine oil coming from deep within the bowels of the earth.

If we cannot trace oil by its name *per se* in the Bible, we must then depend on allusion and synonym, on symbol and type. Since this kind of tracing is subsidiary and not primary

---

[2] Philip Mandelker, "The Search for Oil in the Land of Israel; A Biblical Treasure Hunt" Zion Oil & Gas Company 2006.

in its discovery and process, we must seek the primary trace line. If God did put oil in the sandy bosom of the Promised Land, He had a purpose for doing so. God's purpose would suggest a plan, and if we look hard enough we can discover his plan, and in the process see if there is petroleum present.

CHAPTER THREE

JACOB: THE BEGINNING

Although the unconditional covenant of God was given to Abraham, and it was to him that God promised to, "make of thee a great nation," we will start with Jacob, his grandson. Jacob was the heir of God's promise to Abraham in every way; that is, what he said to Abraham he said to Jacob. The greater part of the Abrahamic covenant was futuristic in manifestation. It was in God's plan from the very beginning to use Jacob as a starting point, a national identity. This was clear even before Jacob was born, as he was yet in Rebekah's womb.

[22]And the children struggled together within her; and she said, If it be so, why am I thus? And she went to inquire of the Lord.

[23]And the Lord said unto her, Two nations are within thy womb and two manner of people shall be separated from thy bowels; and the one people shall be stronger than the other people; and the elder shall serve the younger.

[24]And when her days to be delivered were fulfilled, behold, there were twins in her womb.

[25]And the first came out red, all over like an hairy garment; and they called his name Esau.

[26]And after that came his brother out, and his hand took hold on Esau's heel; and his name was called Jacob....

Genesis 25:22 – 26

The men were as different in their living as they were in their birthing. Esau was rough, an outdoor man. Jacob was smooth, an indoor man.

Later Jacob outmaneuvered Esau, both for his birthright and for his father's blessing. The blessing that Isaac gave Jacob, albeit unknowingly, was essentially the same blessing that Abraham his father had given to him, who had in turn received it from God.

> The name Esau was a pun on the word Edom meaning "red." The name Jacob literally means "heel-snatcher," a Hebrew term for one who supplants, or takes the place of another, either by force or treachery.

Intrigue followed Jacob as he finally got the wife he thought he had bargained for in the beginning. But the wife he loved, Rachel, was barren. Jacob wanted sons more than anything else. Leah, his first wife, the one he didn't even like, bore him a son. Finally, over a period of years and rather capricious family relationships involving his wives and their handmaids, Jacob ended up with twelve sons. Even Rachel, barren for so long, contributed with numbers eleven and twelve, Joseph and Benjamin. It was a good thing she did too, for without Joseph there would be no future for Israel.

Every Sunday school student knows the story of Joseph and his coat of many colors and his brothers' hatred; how he was sold into Egypt as a slave, but by God's intervention was made the number two man in all of Egypt.

Then the famines came in Canaan and drove the children of Israel down to Egypt. Egypt had experienced famine also, but Joseph, under God's direction, had stored more than enough food to last through the famine. The children of Israel were saved from starvation; Jacob and his sons were happily reunited with Joseph; and once again Jacob and his twelve sons were a unit; a nation in embryo.

Jacob Adopts Two Sons

Things went well for Jacob in Egypt, as the Bible testifies: "And Israel dwelt in the land of Egypt, in the country of Goshen; and they had possessions therein, and grew and multiplied exceedingly" (Genesis 47:27). All in all, Jacob lived in Egypt seventeen years before his death. As he was near death he called Joseph unto him:

29...and said unto him, If now I have found grace in thy sight, put, I pray thee, thy hand under my thigh, and deal kindly and truly with me; bury me not I pray thee in Egypt.

30But I will lie with my fathers, and thou shalt carry me out of Egypt, and bury me in their burying place. And he said, I will do as thou hast said.

31...And Israel bowed himself upon the bed's head

Genesis 47: 29 – 31

And it came to pass after these things, that one told Joseph, Behold, thy father is sick; and he took with him his two sons, Manasseh and Ephraim.

Genesis 48:1

Joseph and his two sons went to Jacob's death bed where Jacob had a strange but wonderful surprise waiting for them. First, he blessed Joseph with:

Behold, I will make thee fruitful, and multiply thee, and I will make of thee a multitude of people; and I will give this land to thy seed after thee for an everlasting possession.

Genesis 48:4

Then came the surprise! Jacob, not even seeing Joseph's two sons (for his eyes were weak), told Joseph that he was going to adopt them as his own. Jacob said:

And now thy two sons, Ephraim and Manasseh, which were born unto thee in the land of Egypt before I came unto thee into Egypt, are mine; as Reuben and Simeon, they shall be mine.

Genesis 48:5

Why Would Jacob Adopt His Grandsons?

You might ask: "Why would Jacob want to adopt two sons when he already had twelve? Why adopt them when he was dying?" First and foremost, we are convinced that this was the plan of God, and God directed a dying Jacob to do this. But Jacob's human motivation is clear too. Jacob loved Joseph more than his other sons. He felt partly responsible for Joseph being sold into Egypt as a slave. Lastly, he was so very appreciative of Joseph for saving his family from starvation and then establishing them in Goshen land.

Whatever the motivation was for Jacob's action, the result was dynamic and, as we will see later, strategically important. Ephraim and Manasseh were now to be considered Jacob's sons and would share in the inheritance as full-fledged sons, not once removed grandsons. As a simple matter of fact, Jacob was giving a double blessing to Joseph by issuing a two-for-one stock dividend!

Jacob then put his right hand on Ephraim and his left hand on Manasseh and blessed them. He then turned to Joseph and said:

[21] Behold, I die; but God shall be with you, and bring you again unto the land of your fathers.

[22] Moreover I have given thee one portion above thy brethren, which I took out of the hand of the Amorite with my sword and with bow.

Genesis 48: 21 – 22

Manasseh was put before Jacob's right hand at the place of the
first born; Ephraim was on Jacob's left. Jacob crossed his arms
in order to bless Ephraim with his right hand and Manasseh with
his left. This is the third incidence in Genesis when the blessing
belonging to the eldest son is given to the younger.

In summary, when the children of Israel later would go
in to take possession of their promised land, Joseph would
receive two portions with the names of his sons Ephraim and
Manasseh affixed to them

Jacob's Last Blessing

As Jacob was now very near death, he called all of his
sons together to give out his last blessing. Genesis 49:1
declares this in very interesting fashion:

> And Jacob called unto his sons, and said, Gather
> yourselves together, that I may tell you that which shall
> befall you in the last days![1]

Just imagine, Jacob is going to tell his sons what is
going to befall them in the *"last days,"* and he is speaking
1600 years before Christ, almost four millennia before the last
days!

Jacob proceeds to deal with each son individually in
Chapter 49, but for our purpose we will focus only on Joseph
and his blessing. Look with me at Genesis 49:22: "Joseph is a
fruitful bough, even a fruitful bough by a well; whose
branches run over a wall." Three things deserve notice in this
verse. First, Joseph is to be fruitful. Second, he is a "fruitful
bough by a well" *(very interesting)*. Third, his blessings are so
abundant that they "run over the wall." This phrase tells us
that indeed this blessing of Joseph's was to be plentiful and
abundant. The fruit on the branches would be shared with

---

[1] Exclamation mark author's

those on the outside, those beyond the wall. I take this to mean other nations beyond Israel. Still, Joseph's blessing continues.

CHAPTER FOUR

THE HEAD OF JOSEPH

Blessings? Riches? Could they be the same? Is Joseph to be blessed to the extent that it could be called a national treasure? Has the Bible become an intricate treasure map for wealth that must be discovered in the *"last days"?* (Genesis 49:1). If so, are there clues right here in this chapter that might help us? Let's press on to Genesis 49:25:

> Even by the God of thy father, who shall help thee; and by the almighty, who shall bless thee with blessings of heaven above, <u>blessings of the deep that lieth under,</u> blessings of the breasts, and of the womb:

Most of this verse is self-explanatory, except the phrase: "blessings of the deep that lieth under." What kind of blessing could this be? It says three things: It's a *blessing*, it's *deep*, and it *lieth under*. The verse by itself doesn't give us a real clue. By itself it is too oblique, too veiled.

> "This blessing would be liquid, very deep ... waiting for them, and it would be depressed...The words carry the meaning 'as a mass of water' − not necessarily water .... Besides ... God would somehow, some day use this buried resource in a prophetic way to draw, provide for, and unify His people in the land of promise."[1]

---

[1] Roger Luther, PhD, "Study of Genesis 47 and Deuteronomy 33." 2004

But we already have two things going for us that we can add to this verse. First, we know what treasure of blessing we are looking for – *oil*. Next, we have the clue in verse 22 that states: "Joseph is a fruitful bough, even a bough by a well." Let's put our clues together. We are looking for oil, and oil comes from a well. The main reservoir or pool of oil down under the earth might be the "blessings of the deep that lieth under."

"Too far-fetched," you say? Are we trying to make something fit that doesn't fit? A well could mean a supply of water, or this well could be a symbolic well denoting supply that brings abundance. "It's too hard to even guess what the 'blessings of the deep that lieth under' means. It really doesn't tell us anything. It is too mysterious."

That is right. I would be the first to agree with that kind of reasoning, and with our initial conclusion. We already know that Joseph's blessing is written in code. It is cryptic and needs a key to unlock it. It was given for those days, but it wasn't to be understood until the time of its fulfillment – the "last days." It is evident, however, that these scriptures won't stand by themselves to declare to us, "there is oil in Israel."

Genesis 49:26, the next verse, continues with more of Jacob's blessing for Joseph:

> The blessings of thy father have prevailed above the blessing of my progenitors unto the utmost bound of the everlasting hills: they shall be <u>on the head of Joseph, and on the crown of the head of him that was separate from his brethren</u>.

When Jacob declares here that "The blessings of thy father have prevailed above the blessing of my progenitors," I believe he is referring specifically to Abraham and Isaac. Even though the unconditional covenant of God was first given to Abram (Genesis12:2-3) and perpetuated through his son Isaac, it was Jacob who received the greater manifestation of the promise.

The covenant is brought into focus in Jacob, named Israel. Jacob's name, Israel, was not only to be the name of the "great nation" that God had promised Abram (Genesis 12:2), but Jacob's sons were the tribes, or subsidiary social units, through whom the possessing of the land was to be effected. Indeed, Jacob's blessings did prevail above the blessings of his progenitors even in his own day.

But the rest of verse 26 interests us far more in our treasure hunt! Here Jacob speaks of future blessings with "they shall be" on Joseph's head. He is actually telling us *where* the treasure (blessing) is! Look closely at the words again: "they shall be on the head of Joseph and on the crown of the head of him...." This is our first clue as to where the endowment is, rather than what it is. From this moment on we know that the bonanza we seek (oil) is to be found on Joseph's head. God has, in fact, anointed Joseph's head with oil!

But what does that mean? Is it symbolic of cryptic or both? We know it can't be literal. I personally think that it is mostly cryptic. I feel it is only symbolic in the general sense in the meaning of anointing the head with oil. The Old Testament gives us several instances of this rite. Its usual meaning was to signify authority and blessing being conferred by a higher power. That is what I believe we see here. God is blessing Israel through this anointing of Joseph. However, our goal is not to discover veiled general meanings, but to find specific hidden liquid assets.

So then, if we can rely on the assumption that Genesis 49:26 tells us where the treasure is, what do we do now? It is clear that the verse is cryptic; that is, it is in code. We must unlock the meaning. To do this we must go on to see where this and the other two clues lead us. We must follow the scripture until it reveals to us its hidden meaning. We do have a couple of guides that we can follow personally with our clues. Our guides are named Joseph and Israel: Joseph the family and Israel the land. At this juncture Joseph is our guide.

Jewish tradition states that there are four ways to interpret Holy Scripture. Using the acronym PRDS - "Paradise" (the Hebrew alphabet contains no vowels).

P (Pay - p'shat) – "literal" (literally)

R (Reish - remez) – "hint" or "clue" (prophetically)

D (Dalet - drash) – "homiletic" or "example" (figuratively)

S (Samech - sod) –"secret" (cryptically)[2]

Keeping Joseph in Sight

Armed with our three little clues, let us hurry on to follow Joseph after the death of his father Jacob. Genesis 50: 22 – 26 gives us the scriptural story of what happened:

[22]And Joseph dwelt in Egypt, he, and his father's house: and Joseph lived an hundred and ten years.

[23]And Joseph saw Ephraim's children of the third generation: the children also of Machir the son on Manasseh were brought up on Joseph's knees.

[24]And Joseph said unto his brethren, I die: and God will surely visit you, and bring you out of this land unto the land which he sware to Abraham, to Isaac, and to Jacob.

[25]And Joseph took an oath of the children of Israel, saying, God will surely visit you, and ye shall carry up my bones from hence.

[26]So Joseph died, being an hundred and ten years old: and they embalmed him, and he was put in a coffin in Egypt.

---

[2] Philip Mandelker, personal interview 5 April, 2005.

Following the Sons

And so our guide, so quickly followed, is so quickly gone. We must, of course, follow his sons and their sons as we move ever closer to the mysterious *"blessings"* treasure. But before we grab our biblical spade to dig up another clue, let us consider the importance of Joseph's life from God's perspective. Perhaps we will then be better able to understand the unique role of Joseph in all of this.

Joseph Left a Heritage

Joseph had gone from prisoner to Prime Minister in Egypt. It was strictly providential that Joseph be in this high position at the time of famine so that his people might be preserved.

Yet, we see another strategy of a provident God in getting the Israelites to leave Canaan at that time. They had to have the time and the opportunity to develop a national strength, so that when they took possession of the land they might have the sections properly allotted to the tribes, and thus prevent the tribes as tribes from becoming disintegrated by settling in different parts of the country. It was most important that the tribes be kept together and be properly located (more on this later).

It was also necessary that the Israelites be taken out of Canaan so that they would not mingle and intermarry with the idolatrous races of the people who also dwelled in Canaan. The famine forced them out of Canaan into Egypt where they were put in a separate place called Goshen.

The Hyksos nation had conquered Egypt before this time, and so there was a Hyksos Pharaoh on the throne during Joseph's sojourn there. The importance of this lies in the fact that the Egyptians hated the Hyksos and would have nothing more than was absolutely necessary to do with them. Joseph, a foreigner, was favored by the Hyksos Pharaoh, a foreigner to the Egyptians, and so the idolatrous Egyptians rejected him and his people out of hand. This preserved the children of Israel from associating with them and their paganism. This Egyptian experience was also a fulfillment of prophecy that was given to Abram.

> And he said unto Abram, Know of a surety that thy seed shall be a stranger in a land that is not theirs, and shall serve them; and they shall afflict them four hundred years.
>
> Genesis 15:13

He also promised in verse 14 that "afterward shall they come out with great substance."

Joseph's life was integral in its purity and its power to the preservation, development, and preparation of Israel relative to the possession of the Promised Land. It is because of this, I believe, that God allotted a double portion of land in Canaan to Joseph, and anointed Joseph's head with the oil of blessing and prosperity.

Recapping the Clues

Let us now briefly recap our *clue* scriptures to bring us up to date and prepare us for the next step toward the mysterious X on our treasure map. First we have Genesis 49:22 that tells us that "Joseph is a fruitful bough ... by a well." Could this possibly allude to a fountain of oil that would some day spring up out of Joseph's land?

Second, Genesis 49:25 speaks of the "blessings of the deep that lieth under ...." Is the "deep that lieth under" a great pool of petroleum?

Third, Genesis 49:26 points us to the place of Joseph's blessings. It says that they will be found "... on the head of Joseph, and on the crown of the head of him that was separate from his brethren." This makes it simple, yet hard. We have discovered the place of Joseph's blessings, the top of his head. Now all we have to do is find his head!*

*(Author's note): At this moment you may be mumbling, "This is ridiculous; this sounds like some mad, mad, mad world television script – long on fantasy and nonsense, but short on fact." I couldn't agree more, for that is exactly what I said! One of my biggest problems was this: Is it sensible to think that an ancient civilization would actually write something in code that would not be decoded until modern time? The idea was so remote, but then I thought of the Rosetta Stone.

Consider the Rosetta Stone

Ancient Egypt wrote special messages that were carved in stone. The pyramids of famous Pharaohs provide numerous examples. The cryptic writings are called hieroglyphics (temple writings). Hieroglyphics guarded the treasure of ancient Egypt for millenniums. Not until the key was discovered was the great treasure house opened.

It was 1799 that the key, the Rosetta Stone, was accidentally found. It was someone in Napoleon's invading French army who uncovered the great basalt rock. It was found at the Rosetta mouth of the great Nile River, hence its name. There was a Greek inscription on the Rosetta Stone, and it was this writing that gave the key to the French scholar Champollion who deciphered the Egyptian hieroglyphics. It was so easy to unlock the treasures of millennia *after* the key had been found and applied.

If the ancient Egyptians used the principles of coded language for their own veiled purpose, couldn't God use the same principle (at about the same time in history) for His own purpose? If the Egyptian hieroglyphic key, the Rosetta Stone, was not presented publicly until the 1800's, is it too hard for us to imagine the discovery and presentation of the key to this Bible code in the 1900's? Remember what Jacob said to his sons at the time that he called them together to give them his final blessing: "Gather yourselves together, that I may tell you that which shall befall you in the last days" (Genesis 49:1).

CHAPTER FIVE

ISRAEL, THE LAND

It is time for us to give our guide Joseph a brief rest, and follow for a while our second guide, Israel the land. We remember that Jacob (Israel) made his son Joseph vow that he wouldn't bury him in Egypt, and Joseph, true to his vow, took his father's body back to Canaan and buried him at Machpelah with his father and mother, and grandfather and grandmother.

When it was time for Joseph to die, he demanded an oath also. Joseph's oath was not with one of his sons, but was with the "children of Israel" (Genesis 50:25). He knew that God was going to allow the children of Israel to stay in Egypt only for a prescribed time. When the fullness of time would come, they would leave Egypt and possess Canaan. Joseph, unlike Jacob, was content to have his bones remain in Egypt until that time. Joseph made the Israelites promise that when God did "visit" Egypt to direct them to Canaan, they would take his bones with them that he might also rest with his fathers. The stage is now set for the "Exodus."

> [6] And Joseph died, and all his brethren, and all that generation.
>
> [7] And the children of Israel were fruitful, and increased abundantly, and multiplied, and waxed exceeding mighty; and the land was filled with them.
>
> [8] Now there arose up a new king over Egypt, which knew not Joseph.

⁹ And he said unto his people, Behold, the people of the children of Israel are more and mightier than we:

¹⁰ Come on, let us deal wisely with them; lest they multiply, and it come to pass, that, when there falleth out any war, they join also unto our enemies, and fight against us, and so get them up out of the land.

Exodus 1:6 - 10

From Egypt to the Jordan

The 400 years of Israel's sojourn were almost accomplished. Jacob's family, which had come into Egypt as seventy souls, weak and needy, was now ready to leave as a strong tribal nation.

Moses was born, grew strong, and was schooled by the God of Abraham, Isaac, and Jacob for the arduous task that lay before him. If Joseph, the last great leader of the children of Israel, was the preserver, Moses, the next great leader, was the deliverer. He brought them out of Egypt, through years of futile wandering, to the turbulent Jordan, the river of no return. Moses, now 120 years old, had almost finished his heavenly assignment. He must now pass on the tribal blessings, given hundreds of years ago by Jacob, to the twelve tribes of Israel. It was now time to commission Joshua to lead the tribes in the invasion of Canaan and possess Jacob's inheritance. The land, the tribal blessings; each was dependent on the other,

Once again it is time for us to look closely at our treasure map. We are closer than ever to the mysterious *"X"* and the richest buried treasure in the history of the world!

The Song of Moses

Scripturally our treasure story picks up again in Deuteronomy Chapter 32. This chapter gives us the song of Moses, his swan song, if you please. It was given to all the people for edification and warning. It was his last great sermon. He was, even now, passing the baton of responsibility and authority to Joshua, the next great leader of Israel. For our purposes let us direct our attention to Deuteronomy 32:8 - 13:

[8] When the Most High divided to the nations their inheritance, when he separated the sons of Adam, he set the bounds of the people according to the number of the children of Israel,

[9] For the Lord's portion is his people; Jacob is the lot of his inheritance.

[10] He found him in a desert land, and in the waste howling wilderness; he led him about, he instructed him, he kept him as the apple of his eye.

[11] As an eagle stirreth up her nest, fluttereth over her young, spreadeth abroad her wings, taketh them, beareth them on her wings:

[12] So the Lord alone did lead him, and there was no strange god with him.

[13] He made him ride on the high places of the earth, that he might eat the increase of the fields; and he made him to suck honey out of the rock, and *oil out of the flinty rock:*

The Inheritance of the Nations

The opening statement in verse eight is one of the most dramatic statements in scripture: "When the Most High divided to the nations their inheritance...." As our imagination releases and our thoughts run free, two questions leap forth. *When* did the Most High divide to the nations their inheritance? *What* is a nation's inheritance?

Let's consider the second question first. *What* is a nation's inheritance? I am convinced that it is its land, both the richness of its topsoil, and the wealth deposited deep under the soil. All physical wealth (or inheritance) must come from the land in some form or other, so it seems logical to conclude that the inheritance is the land.

> The original Hebrew text seems to agree that the land is the inheritance. The Hebrew word "chebel" is translated into the English word "lot" in verse nine. "Chebel" literally means "measuring line", "district", "region", or "country". All definitions for "chebel" are geographic in context. This word key will unlock the clues ahead.

It could be argued, I suppose, that people are a nation's inheritance, but this doesn't seem to be very logical. An inheritance is something of value passed on from one generation to another. People do not inherit people. Children don't inherit parents, but rather what the parents possess.

It might also be said that the inheritance of a nation might be a spiritual thing, but this, too, seems unreasonable. God told Moses that He was "I am," not "I was" or "I will be." Each generation and each person of a generation has the responsibility of personally relating to a personal God who dwells in his fullness in that generation. In the Bible some generations are called "sinful"; none are called "righteous." Spiritual kinship is a personal "now," not a national "then."

My conclusion is that a nation's inheritance is its land, or more specifically, its natural resources. In Bible times, during the history of both Testaments, usable natural resources were either on the surface or close to the surface of the land. Some of those resources were lakes, rivers, shallow wells, fertile soil, trees, and even minerals from shallow mines.

The very thought of something valuable being extricated from deep within the earth, such as "the deep that lieth under," was beyond conception. There were no tools, no technological capacity available for such a project. As we have discussed, this technology didn't come until the end of the nineteenth century.

Yet, if the "deep that lieth under" is oil, this kind of chronological timetable would fit perfectly. Remember what Jacob said in Genesis 49:1? He gathered his sons together to tell them what would befall them "in the last days." These are the "last days." So time wise, the fit is a good one.

When Was This Inheritance Given?

Now let us consider the first question. *When* did the Most High divide to the nations their inheritance? Long before Adam was created God was at work in the physical creation. If we count back through the generations of Adam to the time of Adam's creation we end up *circa* 4,000 – 5,000 years before the birth of Christ.

We know that the world is much older than that. In fact, there is evidence that a pre-Adam people existed. We know, by countless fossils, that huge mammals roamed the earth. These animals have been extinct at least for the duration of written history. We know, too, that huge vegetation forests were located in various parts of the world during this pre-history period. But at some moment long ago in the ether-like past of pre-Adam, there was a great cataclysm, a general chaos.

I believe that not only did it happen that way, but that it happened as a direct result of Lucifer being cast down from his exalted place in the heavens to the earth. He was condemned to live on this planet until the time of his ultimate judgment. I am convinced that planet earth came under the scope and span of this judgment, and a catastrophic upheaval of cosmic proportions was set into motion.

How long this lasted isn't even guessable, but when it was finished much of the earth was inside-out. In places, what had been surface was deeply submerged. Great forests, gigantic swamps, giant animals innumerable were volcanically plowed under. What had been formed was now without form. What was alive was now dead. For "the earth was without form, and void, and darkness was upon the face of the deep" (Genesis 1:2).

It seems feasible to think that between Genesis 1:1 and 1:2 there was a chaotic period, this very period that we have just described. Verse one says: "In the beginning God created the heaven and the earth." Verse two continues with the dark statement that the earth was "without form, and void." As God could not create an earth "without form, and void," then something disruptive, something chaotic must have happened between the first and second verses. This could explain the dinosaur fossils, the mountain ranges, the ocean troughs, the earth rifts, the tectonic plates, and the huge lakes of highly compressed animal and vegetable matter couched deep in the earth that we now call petroleum.

> According to the latest seismic studies, geologists believe that Israel's oil lies in 18,000 feet below the surface. This reefal structure is located in lower Triassic and Permian strata geologists believe to be over 200 million years old. God "divided to the nations their inheritance," a long, long time ago.

Jacob Is the Center

Returning now to Deuteronomy 32:8 – 13, let's look at verse nine. In the last part of the verse Moses tells us that "Jacob is lot of his inheritance." For us, the name Jacob is important here because it was with Jacob that we found our first clues, oblique as they were.

Moses, in his death song, almost half a millennium after Jacob, is referring back to Jacob, and to the subject of Jacob's blessing for his sons. Later we will see how Moses actually passes the blessings of Jacob along to the tribes, even expanding the meaning and value of them.

Suffice for us now to see that Moses is discussing Jacob. In verses 9 - 12 he speaks of his special relationship with God; while in verse 13 he gives us our long-awaited next clue - and it is a dandy! Look closely at the last half of verse 13, "...and he made him to suck honey out of the rock, and oil out of the flinty rock!"

Sucking Oil!

Oil! Could it mean olive oil, the only oil known to Moses? No, of course not! It would be absurd to speak of sucking oil out of a certain type of rock when everyone there knew that oil came from crushed olives. Someone might question here: "Isn't it just as absurd to think of sucking honey out of a rock when everyone knew honey came from beehives?" The answer to that is "yes, it is just as absurd," but it doesn't mean *bee* honey;" it means *earth* honey, a synonym for petroleum.

What we have here is a Hebrew parallelism, common in the Bible. Here, honey and oil mean the same thing! The first is symbolic; the second is literal. A simple way to prove this is to locate the verb of the object honey, and of the object oil. Notice that there is one verb, suck, for both objects. Of course, neither honey nor olive oil was sucked into use. Even more interesting is the observation that if you wanted to use the word pump in this context that the Hebrew word here translated suck is the word that you would use.

"Oil out of the flinty rock," remained a phrase of mystery for thousands of years, that is, until 1850, when a process was developed for extracting oil out of shale (flinty rock?).

"Suck" in this passage is "yanaq", the same Hebrew word used for a baby nursing; literally sucking milk from its mother's breast. There are two other Hebrew words that could be translated "suck" but their meanings are closer to "drink up." If

Moses were speaking of "drinking up" olive oil and honey why would use the word for "suckle" rather than the words meaning "to drink up"?

Perhaps he was conveying a different meaning. He had no word for petroleum and he had no concept of the mechanical pump. If Moses wanted to describe "pumping petroleum", concepts of which he hadn't the faintest idea, it's conceivable that the only words he had to describe the picture he had been given by God were "suck honey out of the rock, and oil out of the flinty rock."

Let's say you're willing to consider for a moment that "shemen" *might* be used for petroleum and "yanaq" *might* be used to describe pumping something to the surface. This passage includes "honey". Surely there's not some other Hebrew word for honey?

"D^ebash" is the only Hebrew word for honey. Its literal meaning "to be gummy" or "syrupy", honey was named after its physical properties; not because it was sweet or came from bees. If Moses meant "drink up" olive oil and bees' honey why would he say they would "suckle" them "out of the rock" and "out of the flinty rock?" Using these words individually, a case might be made that Moses was just being poetic; but collectively you've got to wonder if he may have meant something else.

If Moses was trying to accurately describe an understanding given to him by God that, in the last days, an oily, syrupy, sticky substance, maybe amber in color, was to be sucked from the ground and he had no concept of petroleum oil being pumped from deep underground, is it possible that he could have used "yanaq" (to suck) instead of pump and "d^ebash" (gummy syrupy stuff) or "shemen" (oil) instead of petroleum?

So Moses, in his song to the nation Israel, gives us the clearest, the strongest clue yet, in our search for this *buried treasure*. Ah, the Bible, what a treasure map it is! But wait, we mustn't get too excited yet. The best is yet to come. We must resume our search for the mysterious *X*, for it is there that we will dig (drill) for the treasure.

Moses' Blessing

Deuteronomy 33 is the chapter detailing the blessing of Jacob given by Moses. It is here that we shall finally discover our mysterious X.

Verse one is our scriptural first step: "And this is the blessing, wherewith Moses the man of God blessed the children of Israel before his death." This "blessing," this Godly inheritance, is the same blessing given by Jacob just before his death hundreds of years before. It was part and parcel of the covenant made by God with Abram two generations before Jacob.

Jacob's blessing was much more definitive than Abraham's covenant, and now Moses' blessing is much more definitive and precise than was Jacob's. In other words, God didn't give all the information to Abraham or to Jacob, but rather gave as much as was needed at the time. Now, as the children of Israel are actually about to go over Jordan and into the land, he is giving a broader and deeper explanation of the tribal inheritance.

This progressive giving of illumination and knowledge is easier for us to understand when we know that the land is the people's inheritance. For the children of Israel this was graphically true. The closer they got to the land the more they needed to know about its possession, its purpose and its properties.

Deuteronomy 33:6 is where the personal blessing begins. As Reuben is the eldest, it starts with him. Verse seven tells us of Judah's blessing, and verse eight begins the explanation of the blessing of Levi. However, those three tribes are not cogent to our study, so we must nod in recognition and resolutely press on past them. We are about to come upon some very unique and interesting details of our treasure map. The first one is so unobtrusive, so left-handed, that it might go unnoticed by even a careful reader. Let's look at Benjamin, the baby, the youngest of Jacob's brood.

Between His Shoulders?

> And of Benjamin he said, The beloved of the Lord shall dwell in safety by him; and the Lord shall cover him all day long, and he shall dwell between his shoulders.

> Deuteronomy 33:12

Actually there are only two cryptic phrases in this verse; the rest of the verse is easily understood. The first phrase that catches our attention and makes us question is "...and the Lord shall cover him all the day long ...." What does that mean? Is it symbolic or is it cryptic? Is it symbolic, as is the use of "cover" in Psalm 91:4: "He shall cover thee with his feathers, and under his wings shalt thou trust ...?"

I don't think that it is symbolic. I believe that it is both cryptic and literal. This position cannot be proven by verse twelve itself, but we will find that the context of the chapter will provide enough evidence. Sufficient here to state that "to cover" means to put something over the top of something or someone. It sounds like rather a childish explanation, doesn't it? Yet, we will see that it will be more cryptic than pedantic.

The questions continue. What in the realm of common sense or imagination does it mean when it states in verse twelve that "... he shall dwell between his shoulders?" Between whose shoulders will Benjamin be dwelling? The previous phrase says "... and the Lord shall cover him all the day long ...." Should we use grammatical assumption and conclude that Benjamin is to dwell between the Lord's shoulders? This would be very hard to deal with. It's not difficult for us to understand the symbolism of "the hand of the Lord" or "the voice of the Lord," but "between his shoulders" is just too much. Yet, "between his shoulders" has to mean something. Let's see if we can dig it out.

Shoulders...shoulders ... they are a part of the human anatomy; this we know. Just a moment! Didn't we have another part of the anatomy mentioned in one of our clues? Joseph's head! Our third clue (Genesis 49:26) was that "the blessings … shall be on the <u>head</u> of Joseph." Now we have two parts of the anatomy named in our clue search: "head" and "shoulders" - not much to go on, but at least they connect!

Even more difficult to handle is the concept of Benjamin "dwelling" between his shoulders. It doesn't make any literal sense for someone to "dwell" between someone's shoulders. Dwelling supposes a place, a dwelling place. How large would this place have to be? Well, the last numbering of Benjamin's tribe is listed in Numbers 26:41: "These are the sons of Benjamin after their families: and they that were numbered of them were forty and five thousand and six hundred." If the tribe of Benjamin was to dwell between shoulders, it would take some pretty broad shoulders!

The more we look at this the more apparent it becomes that "… between his shoulders" has to do with a portion of land, not a portion of someone's body. The word "shoulders" could only be a hint, a clue to the identification and location of the land that the tribe of Benjamin was about to inherit.

Let's go back, right here, to the question, "whose shoulders?" I don't think it accidental that verse twelve speaks of Benjamin and verse thirteen begins the explanation of Joseph's blessing. The twelve tribes are not listed for blessing in chronological order. I believe it will become apparent later that the continuity of verses twelve and thirteen have a deeper meaning than mere chance. We know that Joseph and Benjamin were full brothers, the sons of Rachel. All of the other brothers were half brothers born of three separate mothers. Still, it appears that the connection of Joseph and Benjamin in the blessing order has a wiser design than the affection of brotherhood. Simply put, it is Joseph's shoulders that Benjamin is to "dwell between." "Ridiculous," you say! Smile on, for the meaning cometh. Ah, ah, just teasing, stay with me.

Joseph's Head Returns

Deuteronomy 33:13-16 describes Joseph's blessing in the new land.

> [13] And of Joseph he said, Blessed of the Lord be his land, for the precious things of heaven, for the dew, and for the deep that coucheth beneath.

> [14] And for the precious fruits brought forth by the sun, and for the precious things put forth by the moon.

> [15] And for the chief things of the ancient mountains, and for the precious things of the lasting hills.

> [16] And for the precious things of the earth and fulness thereof, and for the good will of him that dwelt in the bush: *let the blessing come upon the head of Joseph,* and upon the top of the head of him that was separated from his brethren.

The opening phrases of verse thirteen keep us in focus as we faithfully plod on: "And of Joseph he said, Blessed of the Lord be his land ...." Joseph's "land" has been blessed by God.

How can land be blessed? What is the difference between "blessed" and unblessed land? It seems to me that the only way to "bless" is to makes it rich, both on the surface and under the surface. It also seems to me that that is exactly what God did in his blessing of Joseph's land. Let's take a look at these same verses in the New American Standard Version, as it makes it easier for us to understand this section:

> [13] And of Joseph he said, Blessed of the Lord be his land, With the choice things of heaven, with the dew, and from the deep lying beneath, and with the choice yield of the sun, [14] And with choice produce of the months. [15] And with the best things of the ancient mountains, And with the choice things of the everlasting hills, [16] And with the choice things of the earth and its fulness, And the favor of Him who dwelt in the bush. Let it come to the head of

Joseph, And to the crown of the head of the one distinguished among his brothers.

Deuteronomy 33:13-16 NASB

The Blessings of the Other Brothers

"Jacob's blessing" for Simeon and Levi are non-blessings, judgments. Later, we will see in Deuteronomy 33 that Moses doesn't even mention Simeon's name in his blessing. Levi's not allowed to possess any tribal territory at all but Simeon will finally acquire tribal land.

Since Zebulun, Issachar, and Joseph, and possibly Asher are blessed by Jacob through their land, let's follow these four tribes in Deuteronomy 33 and Moses' blessing. Verse thirteen declares:

And of Joseph he said, Blessed of the Lord be his land, for the precious things of heaven, for the dew, *and for the deep that coucheth beneath.*

"Blessings of the Deep that Lieth Under"

This is very much like Genesis 49:25 which promises "... and by the Almighty, who shall bless thee with blessings of heaven above, blessings of the deep that lieth under ...." There is no doubt that "the deep that lieth under" and "the deep that coucheth beneath" are one and the same.

Because there was no technology to extract anything from "the deep" in the days of Jacob or Moses, neither they nor the children of Israel knew what it was that Joseph was inheriting. It is strong enough for us, however, to use as our fourth clue to lead us to the treasure of oil.

Verses fourteen and fifteen speak of blessings, but more of the variety that would be found on top of the ground, but Deuteronomy 33:16 is a different matter entirely. Look at the last half of the verse: "...let the blessing come upon the head of Joseph, and upon the top of the head of him that was separated from his brethren." We have clue number five, or if you will, a confirmation of clue number three.

Another Hebrew Parallelism

The head of Joseph has indeed returned! It's not the only returnee, for the Hebrew parallelism presents itself once again also. Remember when we discussed Deuteronomy 32:13: "And he made him to suck honey out of the rock, and oil out of the flinty rock?" We have one verb, "suck", but two objects, "honey" and "oil." The action is the same and the objects "honey" and "oil" are the same, really synonyms. Hence, Hebrew parallelism.

> "Two things quickly appear: First, this land blessing for Joseph would be near the top of the land grant and, more specifically, on the part that would correspond to the resting place of a crown on a man's head [directly on the top]. Secondly, this blessing was destined by God for a specific tribe and geographical area set aside by God for a specific divine purpose."[1]

Verse sixteen of chapter 33 has the same construction; a parallelism. "Let the blessing come upon the head of Joseph" parallels with "and upon the top of the head of him that was separated from his brethren." This particular parallelism is much easier to identify than is the one in 32:13, yet is just as important to our treasure hunt.

We have said that the first part of the parallel is usually symbolic and the last part is usually literal. Here, then, we have the symbolism of Joseph's head being anointed with oil by God. The next part of the parallel is much the same as the first, except it designates more precisely just where the blessing (oil) is to be found - "the top of the head." Not the back or the front or the side of the head, but the top is where

---

[1] Roger Luther, PhD, "Study of Genesis 47 and Deuteronomy 33." 2004

the blessing is to be found. A better translation of this word for *"top"* is *"crown"*. The New American Standard Bible uses the word *"crown"* in this verse, as we noticed in the printed translation. Remember that the companion verse of Genesis 49:26 uses *"crown"* instead of *"top"* also. At the moment this does not appear to be very important, but later it will spring forth dramatically as a very necessary part of our map.

Joseph is Represented by His Two Sons

Perhaps you noticed that we left verse seventeen out of our scripture printout in both the King James Version and the New American Standard Bible. This was purposeful. The verse still applies to Joseph, but must be explained separately. The verse says:

> [17] His glory is like the firstling of his bullock, and his horns are like the horns of unicorns: with them he shall push the people together to the ends of the earth: and they are the ten thousands of Ephraim, and they are the thousands of Manasseh.

This verse continues the description of Joseph's blessing, but is somewhat different from the preceding verses in that the blessing is transitioned to Ephraim and Manasseh, his two sons. "His glory is like the firstling of his bullock" is a poetic allusion to this very thing. Finally, the transition is made by the end of verse seventeen with "… and they are the ten thousands of Ephraim, and the thousands of Manasseh."

Jacob did not mention either Ephraim or Manasseh in his blessing in Genesis 49, but Moses here in Deuteronomy 33 has a little different situation. Jacob has already adopted his two grandsons in Genesis 48 so that they would receive Joseph's blessing when Israel returned to the land.

Now that Israel had returned to the land under the leadership of Moses, and he was perpetuating and defining Jacob's original blessing, it was necessary to use Joseph's name in conjunction with that of Ephraim and Manasseh. There was to be no tribal land named *Joseph*. Joseph would receive twice the inheritance of the other brothers, but it would be the names of his two sons that would identify the two portions.

> "It is highly possible, and very probable…that God has additional plans in the future that include the land, the product, and people from the land that was once promised to the sons of Joseph! If God used the productivity and power from the land of Joseph, to conquest and drive away once, he certainly can use it again! Whatever comes out of that land will have might and this might will be of the utmost quality and quantity."[2]

What we must understand from this moment on is that when we speak of Joseph in our hunt for the treasure, we will see Ephraim and Manasseh.

"Rejoice in Thy Going Out"

Jacob's fifth son was Issachar and his sixth son was Zebulun. Leah was the mother of both. As both boys were so close in birth and in life, it is fitting that they be close in their inheritance also. Deuteronomy 33:18 - 19 demonstrates this:

[18] And of Zebulun he said, Rejoice, Zebulun in thy going out; and Issachar, in thy tents.

[19] They shall call the people unto the mountain; there they shall offer sacrifices of righteousness; for they shall suck of the abundance of the seas, and of the treasures hid in the sand.

---

[2] Roger Luther, PhD, ibid

What we see immediately in verse nineteen are the last two phrases. Before we discuss what the verses are saying, let's notice that our friend the Hebrew parallelism has returned once more. In fact, it reminds us of the first parallel we considered (Deuteronomy 32:13), that speaks of sucking "*honey* out of the rock, and *oil* out of the flinty rock." The same word, "suck," is used in both verses.

There was, of course, no word for "pump" in those days, as the idea and the technology for pumping was still thousands of years in the future. Yet, if we were to write these verses today we would say "pump," not "suck."

The next question begs an answer. What is it that one could suck (pump) out of the seas and out of the sand? You don't pump fish out of the seas; they must be netted or hooked. Consider the sand. The idea is just as strange and difficult to comprehend. What in the world could be pumped out of the sand?

I think that the answer on both counts is the same: oil. In recent years offshore oil-drilling has become a normal activity. It looked a little different to begin with, but today seeing an oil rig standing in hundreds of fathoms of ocean water is commonplace. Sucking "of the abundance of the seas" is a *last days* phenomenon.

The sea and the sand, both known petroleum depositories, go together as closely as Zebulun and Issachar in giving us our next vital clue as to where the great treasure is buried. The descendants of Zebulun and Issachar, indeed, will have much to rejoice about.

Oil geologists believe that the lion's share of oil and gas reserves to be discovered in Israel lie offshore in the Mediterranean Sea. A significant amount of Israeli offshore territory is already under oil exploration permit, license, or lease today.

Gad, of the Torn Arm

One of the strangest passages of scripture in the Bible is in Deuteronomy 33:20. Let's look at the whole verse:

> And of Gad he said, Blessed be he that enlargeth Gad: he dwelleth as a lion and teareth the arm with the crown of the head.

The last two phrases are certainly not literal, and they are much too strange to be symbolic, so they must be cryptic. If they are, they fit well with the anatomy code key that we previously introduced.

> The NIV translation may give us a clearer picture of verse 20 and the first part of 21: "Blessed is he who enlarges Gad's domain! Gad lives there like a lion, tearing at arm or head. He chose the best land for himself; the leader's portion was kept for him ...."

We will talk more of this later, when it is time to decipher the code and apply the meaning. Take heart, patient treasure hunters, for the moment draweth nigh.

Asher Dips His Foot in Oil

Deuteronomy 33:24 is a very special verse for us:

> And of Asher he said, Let Asher be blessed, with children; let him be acceptable to his brethren, *and let him dip his foot in oil.*

Here it is, as clear a verse to designate oil in Israel that you could ever ask for. Two things in this verse must not escape our notice. First, the anatomy code is continued: "and let him dip his foot in oil." Next, the word "oil" is used in such a way that we know that it couldn't mean olive oil. It has to mean petroleum. Here someone might ask: "I agree that it couldn't be olive oil - that wouldn't make sense but don't you think that calling it petroleum is stretching the point a bit?" If verse twenty-four was the only verse we had telling us of Asher's oil blessing, we could all ask that same question, but look at verse twenty-five! *"Thy shoes shall be iron and brass*; and as thy days, so shall thy strength be."* Aren't those first seven words marvelous, unique and thought-bending all at the same time? Asher has a foot that is to be "dipped in oil," and has shoes that are to be made of "brass and iron!"

"Dipping the foot in oil points to a land flowing with oil. The text speaks of shoes made of iron and brass and he is to plunge one of these feet into something. Although the [Biblical] Jews would not be miners, the words definitely point to rich natural resources awaiting them in the land... scripture teaches that this tip area of Asher's foot ...contains some of the greatest wealth of all the land promised to Abraham's children and directed specifically to the tribe of Asher. Secondly, part of this wealth is mineral and part of it was (or is) in liquid form."[3]

Do you know that oil derricks are made of brass and iron? Brass against iron does not cause sparks as iron against iron does. So then, the combination of brass and iron is used so that sparks will not ignite an oil well fire!

A few years ago my wife and I were in Singapore. As we boarded the 747 to come home to Los Angeles, we noticed a large group of Americans in the ticket line with us. They were Texans, and they were friendly, but mostly they were happy to be going home.

As we talked with them on the plane we found out the most interesting story of why they were in Singapore. They had just flown into Singapore from Java, they told us, where they had extinguished a huge oil well fire. The fire had been so large and so complicated that the Javanese had been unable to put it out, and had sent for this special crew from Texas.

---

[3] Roger Luther, PhD, ibid

Even then it had taken special equipment, three months of hard work, and thirty million dollars to extinguish the blaze!

It's no wonder that oil companies are so careful about sparks among the oil derricks. Isn't it amazing that Asher's shoes just happen to be made of *"iron"* and *"brass"*, the same metal combination we see used in oil derricks today?

The Fountain of Jacob

Deuteronomy 33:28 explains to us that:

> Israel then shall dwell in safety alone: the fountain of Jacob shall be upon a land of corn and wine; also his heavens shall drop down dew.

This verse tells us three things that can be of help to us in our treasure hunt. The first partial sentence declares: "Israel then shall dwell in *safety* alone." The "then," I imagine, speaks of the time that the treasure is found and the oil discovered. The phrase "… in safety alone" tells us that she will have no allies ready to protect her, yet she will be safe.

This condition squares with Ezekiel 38. Israel's defense, her safety, is, as Ezekiel 38 so dramatically describes, only the Lord God. The next phrase in Deuteronomy 33:28 is "… the fountain of Jacob." What is the fountain of Jacob? Is it the same as Joseph's well (many versions say "fountain") in Genesis 49:22? The answer, I believe, is yes! Jacob's fountain and Joseph's well are one and the same for the following reasons.

1. In Genesis 49 after Joseph's well is mentioned as part of the patriarchal blessing, verse 26 informs us that "The blessings of thy father have prevailed above the blessings of my progenitors … they shall be on the head of Joseph, and on the crown of the

head of him ...." The "blessings" of Jacob are to be found on the head of Joseph!

2. Jacob's fountain "shall be upon a land of corn and wine" (Deuteronomy 33:28). Joseph's blessings include: "... Blessed of the Lord be his land ..." (verse 13); "And for the precious fruits brought forth by the sun ..." (verse 14); "And for the precious things of the earth and fulness thereof ..." (verse 16). Joseph's land would indeed be "a land of corn and wine."

3. Jacob's fountain is to be upon a land where the "heavens shall drop down dew" (verse 28). The last of Joseph's blessings in verse 13 include "... for the dew ...."

We may conclude, then, by biblical evidence, that Joseph's *"well"* and Jacob's *"fountain"* are one and the same.

Is Joseph's Well an Oil Well?

The next question is a little more difficult, and the answer is much more difficult. Yet, it is there, buried deep in the sand of scriptural secrecy.

Is Joseph's "well" – Jacob's "fountain" - an oil well, or even a great oil field? It is my belief and conclusion that, indeed, the latter is a biblical and physical fact. This "fountain" is a great oil field yet to be discovered and developed.

I am convinced that God buried this treasure deep in the heart of the *Promised Land* when "He divided unto the nations their inheritance." This treasure was buried (hidden) and not to be discovered until the *last days* (Genesis 49:1).

The timely discovery of this rich resource would "prolong your days in the land" (Deuteronomy 32:47). It would provide Israel with a powerful position for this perplexing *last days* period. There would now be an overpowering magnetism in Israel for oil thirsty industrial nations. It is even conceivable that these parched national neighbors might come into Israel's front yard to seek a drink at Joseph well!

CHAPTER SIX

BREAKING THE CODE

From the very beginning of our treasure hunt we have looked faithfully through our Bible treasure map for clues that might help us locate the elusive X. After we find the X we will know where to dig. Meticulously we have searched out and listed each clue. Integrated with the clues were hidden meanings and cryptic symbols. As almost every clue referred to the land in some way, we concluded that the land was to be a key for our search.

Then we made a most important discovery: There was a cipher, a code woven in amongst the clues. We called it the anatomy code, for it utilized parts of the human body to symbolize or stand for location.

Let us briefly recap the code discovery. Joseph's head appeared first. The "blessings" were to be found on the *head* of Joseph, yea even upon his crown. Then Joseph's younger brother Benjamin enters the code. It was promised Benjamin that he would dwell safely "between his shoulders." We established that these were Joseph's shoulders. Then we came upon the strange passage that spoke of Gad *"tearing"* his arm with the "crown of the head."

When we got the last anatomy code clue our imaginations just exploded. Asher was going to "dip his foot in oil!" He was going to have shoes made of brass and iron! We knew then that the anatomy code was indeed hiding a great oil discovery. We were sure that if we could break the code, we could find the oil! So, let's break it!

We know that the Promised Land and the anatomy code go hand in hand. They must! The context of scripture won't allow us to believe anything else. The code unlocks the secret that the land has held for millennia. Let's go together to the land.

We Find Joseph's Head

First of all we must locate the head of Joseph in the Promised Land. Remember that Joseph's name won't be attached to any tribal land in Canaan, but the land coming to Joseph would actually be a double portion.

It now seems rather simple, doesn't it? If we cross over Jordan and find the tribal lands of Ephraim and Manasseh we will surely discover Joseph's head! Let's look now at Map 1. This map shows us the Promised Land. It also demarcates the land of each tribe.

Notice how different each portion is from each of the others. It is apparent that the reason for the dividing of the land was not democratic or politically *fair*. The *straight line method* used to divide states such as Colorado, Wyoming, and North and South Dakota was not used.

When you first took at the tribal distribution of land you wonder if anybody was responsible for planning who would settle where. Some tribes have large land holdings, while others are quite small. This is the view of the natural eye, the conclusion of the natural mind. But the division of the land into tribal units was not a natural project; it was a supernatural project. It was God, not man.

Map 1

The Profile of Joseph's Head

Now look at Map 2. This is the same as Map 1 except the lands of Ephraim and Manasseh have been boldly outlined that they might stand out from their neighbors.

Look at the map closely. Do you see it? Do you see Joseph's head? Imagine yourself standing behind Joseph. You are looking at his back. Joseph's head is turned to his left so that you can see a *profile* of his head. He is looking at the Mediterranean Sea. Do you see the crown on his head? Notice the Jordan River. It forms the back of Joseph head.

There are two divisions as Manasseh forms the crown and Ephraim forms the head. Notice the classical styling of the nose as it follows the Mediterranean coastline. Follow on around as the line of the nose turns east, or right, to make the mouth and then the chin.

Map 2

Right here is a good place to say, "Wow Jim, that sure looks like a head with a crown on it, but could it possibly be?"

Joseph's Shoulders

Let's see if we can confirm the conclusion that this is indeed Joseph head, and not a figment of our imagination. Do you remember the scripture concerning Benjamin? It is Deuteronomy 33:12, "And of Benjamin he said, the beloved of the Lord...shall dwell between his shoulders."

We established that "his shoulders" were Joseph's shoulders. Look now at Map 3. Do you see the tribe of Benjamin? Benjamin is dwelling between Joseph's shoulders!

Map 3

This is solid proof that the lines on the map that look like Joseph's head are in fact Joseph's head, for Benjamin is there exactly situated between Joseph's shoulders! Isn't our God amazing?

Now let us look closely at Map 4. This map shows the tribe of Zebulun and Issachar outlined so that we see them clearly. Do you see where they are? They are situated side by side, but more importantly, they are both located on Joseph head!

Map 4

From the very beginning we established that the "blessing," the great oil discovery must be *on* Joseph's head. God had actually anointed his head with oil. Therefore any tribe, such as Zebulun or Issachar that has oil must be located on Joseph's head.

These two tribes according to Deuteronomy 33:19, "... shall suck of the abundance of the seas, and of treasures hid in the sand." Looking at the map we can see that Zebulun only touches the Sea of Galilee, and Issachar doesn't border on any sea. Question - How can these two tribal lands provide "the abundance of the seas" if they aren't next to "seas"?

The answer is easier than the question. If what is being sucked out of Zebulun and Issachar is oil, then the pool of oil is so big that it is "couched" beneath both the Sea of Galilee and the Mediterranean Sea! What a gigantic oil discovery that would be! Everything is fitting fine so far, isn't it?

Gad's Torn Arm

The tribe of Gad now draws our attention. Gad is not an oil-producing tribe, but Gad is useful in helping us with the anatomy code, as well as providing the position of Joseph's head.

Map 5 gives us the bold outline of Gad's territory. Notice that it is on the east side of the Jordan River. Actually two and a half tribes held territory on the east of Jordan. Manasseh, because of her size, was given land on both sides of the Jordan. So then, we say that half of Manasseh's tribe is on each side of the river. Reuben and Gad were located entirely on the east side.

Looking at Map 5, observe that Gad has a long section of land that proceeds north following up the line of the Jordan River. This *arm* of land is *torn* by the jagged line of the Jordan. The crown of the head of Joseph actually tears the line of the arm of Gad's land.

Let's take another look at Deuteronomy 33:20: "And of Gad he said, Blessed be he that enlargeth Gad: he dwelleth as a lion, and teareth the arm with the crown of the head." The second phrase of the verse "… Blessed be he that enlargeth Gad" is speaking of Manasseh, for it is through Manasseh's natural land flow that the arm of Gad's land is extended (enlarged).

Map 5

Manasseh, of course, is the "crown of the head" that "teareth the arm" of Gad's tribal territory. Isn't that something special? The anatomy code is even helpful to us in a secondary support!

Asher Dips His Foot in Oil!

And now for the really big one! Let's zero in on the tribe of Asher. Deuteronomy 33:24 says, "And of Asher he said, Let Asher be blessed with children; let him be acceptable to his brethren, and *let him dip his foot in oil*."

Map 6

Map 6 shows us the borders of Asher's land. As you look at it do you see that the land is shaped like a long leg? The top of the leg is north and the contour moves from north to south. The front of the leg faces the Mediterranean Sea to the west, while the back or calf of the leg borders Naphtali and Zebulun.

Isn't it just too amazing that Asher's foot, which is to be dipped in oil, is on the "head of Joseph, yea and on the crown of the head of him who was separate from his brethren" (Genesis 49:26)?

How much oil will Asher dip his foot into? It has to be an enormous field of petroleum, for the oil derricks will be so close that an airplane flight over Asher's foot would give the impression that he was wearing a shoe made of iron and brass (Deuteronomy 33:25).

What a dramatic and eloquent picture! The portion of land that looks like a foot, which is connected to the portion of land that looks like a leg, will dip into a pool of oil so enormous that it is beyond our imaginings. The foot will wear a shoe made of non-shoe material, iron and brass! Wow! Genesis 49:20 will be fulfilled abundantly: "Out of Asher his bread shall be fat ...." The word for fat in this verse is easily translated "oil."

About Maps

Look in the back of almost any Bible or in any Bible Atlas and you'll find a map of the ancient territories of the twelve tribes of Israel similar to the maps in this chapter.

One thing you will notice is that the borders between the tribes (if there are any borders at all) are not exactly the same as the borders on the maps in this chapter. In fact, if you compare maps between Bibles and Atlases, you'll find that none of the tribal borders on any of the maps are exactly the same.

The reason for this apparent discrepancy is that historical territorial information for the era is not exacting and sometimes one piece of historical data contradicts another. For example one historic record may place an ancient city in a specific location and another may place the same city in a different location.

Placement of exact borders on a map of ancient Israel often is at the discretion and historical interpretation of the map's cartographer.

Don't be too alarmed if the map in your Bible shows Joseph's crown riding lower on his brow, or if Asher's foot is turned to the left instead of the right. Every map agrees with the general geographic location and shape of the tribal boundaries.

Considering the thousands of years that have transpired since the children of Israel entered into Canaan and the land's continual history of conquest, destruction and change, this agreement of geographic location and configuration provides overwhelming evidence of the anthropomorphic connection of the land to the scriptures.

CHAPTER SEVEN

A "P.S." ON JACOB'S BLESSING

We have discussed at great length the blessing that Jacob gave to his sons as he lay dying in Egypt. Our focus has been on the part of the blessing that had to do with oil and its discovery. There is another piece of information concerning Jacob's blessing that fits in very nicely with our study. Let me share it with you.

Turn your mind biblically back to the time and place where Jacob himself received the "blessing" from his father Isaac. The account is found in the twenty-seventh chapter of Genesis. Isaac was old and he was anticipating his death. He asked his oldest son, Esau to come in to him that he might ask of him a special request. Isaac wanted to taste fresh venison again before he died. Esau, the man of the field, was a great hunter, and he hastened to the hunt to do his father's bidding.

While Esau was gone, Jacob, having been informed of the situation by his mother, impersonated Esau and tricked his father into giving *him* the blessing (Jacob had already bartered Esau out of his birthright!).

Birthright and Blessing were, by tradition connected to the firstborn son. The birthright of the firstborn included a double portion of the father's estate, including the responsibility to care for any unwed daughters and the widow or widows of the deceased. Essentially, the firstborn son took over as head of the family and the family's possessions. The blessing was also, by tradition given to the firstborn son.

The blessing was more of a spiritual inheritance, passed down from father to son. The blessing dealt more with sacred relationships and the promise of "good things to come." The right of the firstborn son to these benefits wasn't guaranteed. They could be traded (as with Esau and his birthright for a bowl of soup), given up voluntarily, by deception (as with Jacob and his father's blessing) or taken away at the discretion of God or of the patriarch (as with Ishmael and Isaac).

The blessing not going to the firstborn, however, was outside of tradition and a rare occurrence. The fact that it happened in four consecutive generations (Isaac, Jacob, Joseph, and Ephraim) must mean that God's hand and sovereignty were at work to enact some plan beyond the scope of these men and their traditions.

"The Fatness of the Earth"

The first part of Isaac's blessing that he unknowingly gave to Jacob is the center of our attention. It is found in Genesis 27:28: "Therefore God give thee of the dew of heaven, and *the fatness of the earth* ...." In the Hebrew this literally means "the oil of the ground"! Isn't that intriguing?

But we are not through with this part of our story yet! Esau comes back from the hunt to give his father the fresh venison and finds out that Jacob has bested him again. Verse thirty-four says: "And when Esau heard the word of his father (that Jacob had tricked him and the blessing would stand), he cried with a great and exceeding bitter cry, and said unto his father, Bless me, even me also, O my father."

Esau continued to weep bitterly before his father, asking him if there wasn't some kind of blessing that Isaac might yet give him. Verse thirty-nine gives us Isaac's answer: "...Behold, thy dwelling shall be the fatness of the earth ..."

(the oil of the ground). Isaac uses the same phrase, "the fatness of the earth," both in Jacob's and in Esau's blessing.

What does this show us about these two men, and more importantly, about the nations formed out of them? Let's look at Esau first. Esau was renamed Edom because of his redness (Genesis 25:25-30). As you look at the map of the Middle East during the time of the dividing of the twelve tribes, you can see Edom (also Idumea) as a territory beginning at the Dead Sea and extending south in a fan shape. It was to be known as Arabia.

Today Edom (Esau) is Arabia. Isaac's blessing to Esau has been fulfilled for Esau is indeed *dwelling* on "the fatness (oil) of the earth." Who has more oil (fatness) than Arabia? At this writing the world must answer *"nobody"*. But praise God, we know differently! Jacob has more oil, a lot more oil, and one day the world will know it to the greater glory of God.

> Saudi Arabia, as of 2006 had 262.3 billion barrels of proven oil reserves. Esau's children, the Saudis, produce about 10 million barrels of oil per day.[1]

A note for you geology buffs: The Dead Sea is at the bottom of the earth rift *(tear)* that comes up through the Sinai. Tectonic forces could have actually squeezed the oil, like squeezing a toothpaste tube, down into Arabia. Wouldn't it be something if a latter-day earthquake in Arabia forced the oil *(toothpaste)* up the Jordan River *(tube)* fault line? It could go all the way up to the top of Joseph's head.

Let's Recap

Let us now briefly sum up to see *what* we have found, and *where* it is found. Jacob and Moses teamed up to bless the

---

[1] *Oil & Gas Journal,* Vol. 104, No. 47 (Dec. 18, 2006). From: U.S. Energy Information Administration

children of Israel with blessings that would help fulfill God's covenant with Abraham. The blessings were to be realized *after* Israel had possessed the land and divided it up into prescribed tribal territories.

Some of the blessings were to be received a *long time* after the demarcation of the land (Genesis 49:1). These "last days" that Jacob spoke of in Genesis 49:1 are the very days that we are living in now. We are now, and will be later, the eyewitnesses of the fulfillment of God's covenant with Abraham. This is especially important to born-again Christians who are in truth the "seed" of Abraham, and "heirs according to the promise" (Galatians 3:29).

When Will This Oil Be Found?

As I write these words, I know two things concerning this question. The first thing I know is that oil *has not* been discovered yet. The second thing I know is that oil *will be* discovered sometime in the years to come. The discovery could be at any time.

It is no secret that the modern state of Israel desperately needs Jacob's blessing right now. Her oil dependency on other nations makes her vulnerable both economically and militarily. With the international power blocs saying "no" to her oil needs, and a national inflation rate that is unmanageable, how many more years could it be?

Since the words above were originally penned in 1981 a great deal has changed but the overall situation remains much the same. Twenty-six years of oil exploration, geological testing, and prayer have transpired. As we will see in Book II, many explorers searching for Israel's treasure have come and gone. The geological proof is in, the first back bays of an oil sea have been tapped; today we are witnessing the beginning of this prophecy's fulfillment. Israel needs oil independence and the safety of autonomy more than ever. The message of Israel's oil is far more relevant today than ever before.

CHAPTER EIGHT

GOG AND MAGOG

When the great oil fields that anoint Joseph's head *are* discovered, and the neighboring nations recognize the impact of the discovery, what will they say? What will they do? As far as the Arab nations are concerned, it won't make much difference what they say or do, as they are extremely bellicose anyway.

However, there are other nations in that part of the world that would be extremely interested in a new oil field discovery. The Russian bear, a near neighbor of Israel, is foraging even now for new "earth honey" in which to dip its hungry paw. The bear must feed her brood that guards her European hunting grounds. She hungers for *honey* and thirsts for blood.

The Hooks in the Jaws

Ezekiel thirty-eight begins with:

[1] And the word of the Lord came unto me, saying,

[2] Son of man, set thy face against Gog, the land of Magog, the chief prince of Meschech and Tubal, and prophesy against him.

[3] And say, Thus saith the Lord God; Behold, I am against thee, 0 Gog, the chief prince of Meshech and Tubal:

The line is drawn quickly and forcefully. God is setting himself against Gog and Magog! There is no doubt about the identification of Gog. It is Russia. If you happen to be using an ASV, NASB or a Jerusalem Bible translation instead of the King James Version, you will see the word "Rosh" used in place of "Gog." Magog speaks of some of the tribes or sub-nations that have evolved from and with the chief prince of Meshech (Moscow) and Tubal (Tobolsk).

Russia is a conglomerate of these sub-nations. Their original springing forth can be traced all the way back to Genesis 10:2. This verse gives us the Sons of Japheth, who was a son of Noah. They are listed as: "The sons of Japheth, Gomer and Magog, and Madai, and Javan, and Tubal, and Meschech, and Tiras."

"The Jewish tradition of Gog and Magog is quite distinct from the Bible and describes 70 national angels, some of which have fallen and others are still with God. The Biblical prophecy says that Gog – who in the tradition is the angel of the nation called Magog – will be defeated after he leads an army to attack Israel from the four corners of the land. This angel therefore represents the spirit of anti-Semitism."[1]

So, Russia and God will be literally at sword point. Ezekiel thirty-eight, verse three says: "...I am against thee, 0 Gog." We know that Russia has been *against* God since 1917 and the communist revolution.

The great confrontation will finally take place even as these verses go on to describe it:

[4] And I will turn thee back, and put hooks into thy jaws, and I will bring thee forth, and all thine army, horses and horsemen, all of them clothed with all sorts of armor, even a great company with bucklers and shields, all of them handling swords:

---

[1] Wikipedia

[5] Persia, Ethiopia, and Libya with them; all of them with shield and helmet:

Ezekiel 38:4-5

Verse four tells us that God *Himself* is going to bring about this great confrontation. "I will … put hooks into thy jaws, and I will bring thee forth …." The Russian bear will have "hooks" put into her jaws that she may be drawn southward into Israel.

What do you think these "hooks" will be? The word "hooks" is most certainly symbolic of something that has a drawing effect on Russia to bring her into this mighty confrontation. Do you think possibly that this "hook in the jaw" could be the newly-discovered oil fields of Israel?

It is Only a Matter of Time

Computer workups tell us that the Russian republics are in a state of diminishing returns. Part of this is attributable to the breaking up of the USSR into independent and separate smaller republics.

Oil reserves are lower and have been kidnapped by inter-republic competition. If this scenario is correct, then it would seem feasible to think that Russia and some of her allies might consider the new oil fields an irresistible drawing attraction.

> Russia's "proven reserves" are at 60 billion barrels. Her current daily production is over 10 million barrels per day. If she keeps production in pace with the current rate of increase in demand, Russia's reserves will be gone by 2021.[2]

---

[2] http://www.eia.doe.gov/emeu/cabs/Russia/Oil.html

We see three of her allies in verse five. They are Persia (Iran), Ethiopia, and Libya. At this writing Iran has not aligned herself with Russia, but it is only a matter of time before she does. Since the tragic American hostage situation, Iran has little political or economic involvement with the United States in particular, or the West in general.

Having been semi-industrialized and semi-modernized by the late Shah Pahlavi, she must ally herself with someone who can supply her with the industrial and military material to keep on going. Where she was almost completely supplied by the United States, she must now look for another *"complete"* supplier. Russia is the only viable candidate who stands ready to do that. So, as I said, it is only a matter of time.

New Zealand Herald, July 24, 2007

"China and Russia are seeking to cement their strategic partnership and create a multi-polar world in which the United States will find it much more difficult to dominate international affairs....

Founded in Shanghai in 2001, the [Shanghai Co-operation Organisation] has six full members: China, Russia and four former Soviet republics in Central Asia, Kazakhstan, Kyrgyzstan, Tajikistan and Uzbekistan....

Neighbouring states are flocking to associate themselves with the group at the highest possible level. Among them is Iran, seeking protection and allies in its battle to fend off pressure from the US, Europe and other countries that suspect it is secretly trying to develop atomic weapons in the guise of a peaceful nuclear programme ... its hardline President Mahmoud Ahmadinejad is scheduled to attend the August 16 summit in Bishkek, Kyrgyzstan, as a distinguished guest, intensifying speculation Tehran may join the group as a full member."[3]

3

http://www.nzherald.co.nz/section/2/story.cfm?c_id=2&objectid=10453331

Ethiopia is a Russian satellite state. For many years Ethiopia was pro-Western, but Soviet saturation has now set in.

> Ethiopia and Russia have signed a diplomatic and service passport free visa agreement. Ambassador Lipnyakov on his part said the agreement would be instrumental in further strengthening the cooperation between Ethiopia and Russia.[4]

Libya is a country large in land, small in people, poor in agriculture and industry, and rich in oil. Libya has come under Russian influence also. In 1974, Russia brought pressure to bear upon Colonel Moamar Gaddafi, the Libyan leader, to expel the Americans from their bases in Libya, charging them with being imperialists. As soon as the American *"imperialists"* moved out of the Libyan bases, the Russian imperialists moved in!

That was in 1974. In 1978, Russian and Cuban troops helped the *"revolutionary army"* bring Ethiopia in line with Russian communism. It was in 1979 that the American hostages were taken captive in Iran. They were released in 1981. The dates sort of move along together as if someone or something is orchestrating a concert for conflict.

> **Libya nears arms deal with Russia, 17 May 2007**
>
> Libya and Russia are believed to be close to signing an arms agreement for the sale of Russian fighter aircraft and air-defence systems to Tripoli under a USD2.2 billion deal.[5]

The Last Days

Isn't it amazing how a biblical prophecy given in the sixth century before the birth of Christ demonstrates such

---

[4] Addis Ababa, December 12, 2002 (ENA)
[5] http://www.janes.com/news/defence/business/jdw/jdw070517_1_n.shtml

definitive accuracy twenty centuries after his birth? It is a graphic demonstration for us that these are the "last days," or as Ezekiel says, "the latter years." I could not have written these words thirty-five years ago with any suggestion that these three countries would be in Russia's camp, for at that time there was not even a hint that they ever would be! Look at the years together:

1973 - Yom Kippur War and oil embargo

1974 - Libya goes Russian

Ethiopia follows in 1978

1979-81 Iran moved toward the hammer and sickle

Just think of it!

> On the surface, Russian-Israeli relations have warmed. Israel currently buys 90% of its foreign oil from Russia and Caspian region countries. If Israel were to quit Russia as a major oil customer overnight, the relationship would immediately cool. But beneath the surface the Russian alliance with Persian Gulf and North African nations has matured into a mutual self-help pact. Russia supplies the PLO and Persian Gulf countries with arms and war materiel. The Arab nations provide much needed cash to Russia.

Yet these three nations are not the only allies of Russia that will move against Israel's "unwalled villages." Ezekiel 38:6 declares that "Gomer, and all his bands; the house of Togarmah of the north quarters, and all his band," will also be included in this great military campaign.

Gomer is the ancient name for Germany, while Togarmah is the ancient name for Turkey. East Germany, of course, had been Soviet-dominated since 1945. West and East Germany are now joined as one and will move in as a national unit - just as the singular name *"Gomer"* implies. There is no East Gomer and West Gomer!

> For historical reasons, Germany and Russia are destined to have a special relationship.... Opinion polls indicate that Russian elites regard Germany as a true friend and advocate in the West. Moscow does not consider Germany, a nonnuclear state, to be a geopolitical rival in the post-Soviet space as it does, for instance, the United States. Germany is Russia's most important foreign trading partner....
>
> Correspondingly, German elites enjoy their country's role as an advocate of European interests with Russia, particularly in the economic field and often as mediator between Russia and the United States.[6]

Turkey, like Iran, is situated on Russia's southern border, and will give way to her pressure.

> **Turkey-Russia relations**
>
> Given their dynamically growing economic co-operation, the leaders of Turkey and Russia are now working for closer political dialogue to match.
>
> For centuries, Turkey and Russia have been rivals for regional supremacy. Recently, the two countries have realised that friendly relations are in the interest of them both. Accordingly, co-operation rather than rivalry appears to dominate their ties. This development has been welcome by the EU, which sees these countries as the two largest imponderables on the European horizon.[7]

What is the Timetable?

When will all this happen? When we consider the frequency of these recent dates, it appears as if it could be soon. Ezekiel 38:8 declares:

---

[6] http://www.twq.com/07spring/docs/07spring_rahr.pdf
[7] Euractive.com May 2, 2005

> After many days thou shalt be visited: in the latter years thou shalt come into the land that is brought back from the sword; and is gathered out of many people, against the mountains of Israel, which have been always waste: but it is brought forth out of the nations, and they shall dwell safely all of them.

What an informative verse! It gives us five hints as to when this huge military machine is to move into Israel.

First, it will be "after many days." The prophetic day is a year, and so it reads more correctly "after many years." This has already happened; many years have passed.

Second, it is to be "in the latter years." If we study Matthew twenty-four to give us the "signs of the times," we may conclude that we are now in the "latter years."

Third, Russia and her allies are to come into a "land that is brought back from the sword!"

Fourth, the nation is to be "gathered out of many people." Israel, today, is exactly that: She is a new nation literally "gathered out of many people."

Fifth, the enemy from the north is to descend upon the "mountains of Israel, which have been always waste…." This waste land was a result of the "seven times" judgment spoken of in Leviticus 26:27-45. Verse thirty-three sums it up briefly:

> And I will scatter you among the heathen, and will draw out a sword after you: and your land shall be desolate, and your cities waste.

Israel's wasteland was a direct result of God's judgment.

The Wastes Shall Be Builded

On the other hand, God promised that he would reverse the process when he restored Israel. Ezekiel 36:6-11 is the declaration of this promise:

> [6] Prophesy therefore concerning the land of Israel, and say unto the mountains, and to the hills, to the rivers, and to the valleys, Thus saith the Lord God; Behold, I have spoken in my jealousy and in my fury, because ye have borne the shame of the heathen:

> [7] Therefore thus saith the Lord God; I have lifted up mine hand, Surely the heathen that are about you, they shall bear their shame.

> [8] But ye, O mountains of Israel, ye shall shoot forth your branches, and yield your fruit to my people of Israel; for they are at hand to come.

> [9] For, behold, I am for you, and I will turn unto you, and ye shall be tilled and sown:

> [10] And I will multiply men upon you, all the house of Israel, even all of it: and the cities shall be inhabited, and the wastes shall be builded:

> [11] And I will multiply upon you man and beast; and they shall increase and bring fruit: and I will settle you after your old estates, and will do better unto you than at your beginnings: and ye shall know that I am the Lord.

Israel today is an agricultural wonder. Land that was desert thirty years ago thrives today with incredibly diverse agricultural products managed under the world's most advanced horticultural systems. No other country matches the intensity and diversity of Israel's agricultural output.

"Thou Shalt Think an Evil Thought"

The five things that we have just mentioned are not in a future time frame. These conditions and situations already exist. The only thing that speaks of the future in Ezekiel 38:8 is the first sentence, "After many days thou shalt be visited: in the latter years ...." This refers to "Gog and Magog" being "visited" by the Lord God and drawn down into Israel toward Judgment. The next three verses, nine through eleven, describe the power and the malice of Gog:

> [9]Thou shalt ascend and come like a storm, thou shalt be like a cloud to cover the land ...

> [10]... at the same time shall things come into thy mind, and thou shalt think an evil thought:

> [11]And thou shalt say, I will go up to the land of unwalled villages ... to them that are at rest, that dwell safely... without walls ... neither bars nor gates....

What is Gog's thinking at this point? What evil thought has come into his mind? Ezekiel 38:12 has the answer:

> To take a spoil, and to take a prey; to turn thine hand upon the desolate places that are now inhabited, and upon the people that are gathered out of the nations, which have gotten cattle and goods, that dwell in the midst of the land.

Look at the first four words of verse twelve: "To take a spoil...." Is it coincidental that the last three letters of *spoil* spell *oil*? It may or may not be prophetic, but it is interesting, isn't it? It is inconceivable that this great invasion force would risk international repercussions for just "cattle and goods." Verse thirteen speaks of gold and silver, but this can't stand by itself either. If Gog was chiefly interested in cattle and goods, and silver and gold, then the attack would have to be directed against another country. Israel is not even moderately wealthy in these liquid assets. It would be like Little Red Riding Hood's wolf invading Mother Hubbard's cupboard.

But what if...? What if there is an enormous oil discovery "in the midst of the land?" Now that is a reason for an invasion of this magnitude! This would answer some of the questions that have arisen. Why would a community of nations as obviously gigantic as Russia need allies to invade a country as tiny as Israel? Why attack at this particular time? Why not use nuclear weapons instead of conventional weaponry?

At this moment we can only speculate what the "evil thought" of Gog's really is, that is, what the motivation behind it is to be. However, it is no secret what the heavenly reason is. It is disclosed in the sixteenth verse:

> And thou shalt come up against my people of Israel, as a cloud to cover the land; it shall be in the latter days, and I will bring thee against my land, that the heathen may know me, when I shall be sanctified in thee, O Gog, before their eyes.

"So, let's add things up, shall we? An Israeli oil strike would bring down the wrath of the Islamic world, threaten Russia's plans to use its own oil as a future strategic weapon, and earn Israel a new favored status among the Europeans, bringing all the players in Ezekiel's Gog-Magog invasion to center stage at the same time."[8]

The World Sees God's Holiness

The Lord God Jehovah is going to be sanctified before the entire world. Gog represents internationally-organized evil, and his defeat will represent the defeat of this internationally-organized evil.

The remainder of Ezekiel thirty describes the wrath and judgment of God on Gog and the allied invasion force. God uses both natural and supernatural weapons against Gog. The slaughter is indescribable. Blood colors the mountains

---

[8] Jack Kinsella

and covers the plain. Destruction is utter. *Defeat* can not describe the situation. Only one-sixth of the invasion force survives to limp home and testify to the power of Israel's God.

CHAPTER NINE

WHAT ABOUT ARMAGEDDON?

As awful as the battle and destruction between Gog and God is, it is not the battle called Armageddon. Some feel that the battle of Gog is the first battle between God and the national world systems in the latter years.

Ezekiel 39:9 teaches that the weapons left on the battlefield by Gog's defeated armies will require seven years to burn. This figure offers speculation that the Gog invasion is the trigger for the seven-year tribulatory period spoken of by Daniel and John. Whether this is true or not remains to be seen, but the time of Armageddon's horror is fixed.

Revelation 16:16 tells us of this dramatic and apocalyptic battlefield. The word "Armageddon" means the "Mountain of Megiddo." In Old Testament times there was a city of Megiddo located on the "great plain," or plain of Megiddo.

"Throughout history Megiddo and the Jezreel Valley have been Ground Zero for battles that determined the very course of civilization. It is no wonder that the author of Revelation believed Armageddon, the penultimate battle between good and evil, would also take place in this region!"[1]

---

[1] The Battles of Armageddon, Eric H. Cline

This historic battleground is located between the Galilean hills and the mountains of Israel. It was here that Barak defeated the Canaanites, and Gideon the Midianites. The battle of Armageddon is really more of a war than a battle.

Not only will soldiers be gathered at Megiddo, but also in the south and central parts of the Holy Land. God declares that His sword "shall be bathed in heaven: behold it shall come down upon Idumea (Edom)..." (Isaiah 34:5). Edom is in the south. Joel 3:2 tells us that it is in the valley of Jehoshaphat that God will gather the nations and plead for his people. Some experts feel that the valley of Jehoshaphat is in central Palestine somewhere between Jerusalem and the Jordan River. Revelation 14:20 says:

> And the winepress was trodden without the city, and blood came out of the winepress, even unto the horse bridles, by the space of a thousand and six hundred furlongs.

The blood will be five feet deep for the length of 200 miles! That is the approximate length of Israel today. This war of Armageddon will cover the entire land. Who is it that will be fighting in this terrible war?

Power Blocs of Nations

The Bible tells us that there are international power blocs, or groups of countries that will come against Israel. There are four of these groups, or power blocs, and they come from each direction of the compass.

The northern group contains Russia and her selected allies that we have already discussed in the context of Ezekiel 38. It appears that this battle begins the tribulation period. Although the Russian invasion seems to be part and parcel with this furious flurry of end-time battles, it is also treated separately in scripture.

Daniel chapter 2 tells us of the western confederacy that will move against Israel. It is a group of countries that will represent the old Roman Empire. Daniel, interpreting King Nebuchadnezzar's dream, calls this power bloc "the fourth kingdom." Daniel himself has a dream that is described for us in the seventh chapter of Daniel. It expands Nebuchadnezzar's dream. Daniel 7:7 explains:

> After this I saw in the night visions, and behold a fourth beast, dreadful and terrible, and strong exceedingly; and it had great iron teeth: it devoured and brake in pieces, and stamped the residue with the feet of it: and it was diverse from all the beasts that were before it; and it had ten horns.

The interpretation of this part of the dream is given in Daniel 7:23, 24:

> [23]Thus he said, the fourth beast shall be the fourth kingdom upon earth, which shall be diverse from all kingdoms, and shall devour the whole earth, and shall tread it down, and break it in pieces.
>
> [24]And the ten horns out of this kingdom are ten kings that shall arise: and another shall rise after them...."

The Revived Roman Empire

As we noted, the fourth kingdom was the old Roman Empire, but the ten kings are ten countries that came "out of the kingdom." This "revived" Roman Empire is the power bloc that will come from the west.

There are those today who believe that this ten nation federation comes out of the European Common Market. The Common Market had its beginning on January 1, 1958, with the six countries of West Germany, Belgium, France, Italy,

Holland and Luxembourg as charter members. The three nations of Great Britain, Ireland and Denmark were added on January 1, 1973. The tenth nation, Greece, was officially received into active membership on January 1, 1981. However, the number of members is still in ebb and flow.

> The European Common Market evolved in 1992 into the European Union. Today the E.U. includes 28 member countries. In addition to the ten countries above, Austria, Bulgaria, Cyprus, Czech Republic, Estonia, Finland, Hungary, Iceland, Latvia, Lithuania, Malta, Norway, Poland, Portugal, Slovakia, Slovenia, Spain and Turkey are EU members today.

Is the stage now set for the ten horns to fulfill prophecy? The Bible; teaches that three of these horns will be subdued by another who rises "after." He will proceed to take leadership of the entire confederacy, and then move against the most High God. He will "speak great words against the most High, and shall wear out the saints of the most High..." (Daniel 7:25). Could the Common Market develop into this?

Yes, of course it could. There are those in Europe who have been looking for a superman kind of leader for years. Henri Spaak, an early Common Market leader, stated it graphically, perhaps prophetically. He announced:

> We do not want another committee, we have too many already. What we want is a man of sufficient stature to hold the allegiance of all people, and to lift us out of the economic morass into which we are sinking. Send us such a man and be he god or devil, we will receive him!

> Don't worry too much about the EU now including more than ten countries, disqualifying it from being the *"ten kings"* mentioned in Daniel. The original ten countries are the only full members of the EU. The other "newcomers" are relegated to *"Associate"* or *"Observer"* roles.

The Kings of the South and East

The *"king of the south"* heads the southern power bloc. Egypt is the leader, but there will undoubtedly be Arab countries in close alliance with her. Egypt, although oil poor, has been historically the leader of the Arab countries.

> The Arab Persian Gulf and North African Muslim nations have become radically anti-West (U.S.) and have always been radically anti-Israel. Egypt, playing the role of moderate since Camp David and the return of the Sinai no longer speaks to the sentiments of the Muslim nations.

The fourth and last power bloc is what the Bible refers to as the "kings of the east." We can't say much about this, for the scripture only mentions it twice (Daniel 11:44 and Revelation 16:12). However, it seems that they must represent China, India and Japan, as well as other minor states.

> Asia, including China, India, and Korea, is the largest emerging market the world has ever seen. As it grows into maturity, its appetites and power will be capable of eclipsing every other national group on the planet.

The Whole Earth Is Against Zion!

It seems as if all four corners of the earth have been armed and are marching toward Zion! They come to represent by force their own economic interests. They come to do battle against any adversary that would keep them from their quest, their goal. They are prepared to do battle against each other, but then something turns their fury toward God and His people.

Christ's Triumphant Return

This is the time of the Lord's triumphant return in power and great glory. The military might of the world is aligned against him. The Beast and the False Prophet await the calamity of the coming Christ. John describes it in Revelation 19:11 – 21:

¹¹And I saw heaven opened, and behold a white horse; and he that sat upon him was called Faithful and True, and in righteousness he doth judge and make war.

¹²His eyes were as a flame of fire, and on his head were many crowns; and he had a name written, that no man knew, but he himself.

¹³And he was clothed with a vesture dipped in blood: and his name is called The Word of God.

¹⁴And the armies which were in heaven followed him upon white horses, clothed in fine linen, white and clean.

¹⁵And out of his mouth goeth a sharp sword, that with it he should smite the nations: and he shall rule them with a rod of iron: and he treadeth the winepress of the fierceness and wrath of Almighty God.

¹⁶And he hath on his vesture and on his thigh a name written, KING OF KINGS, AND LORD OF LORDS.

¹⁷And I saw an angel standing in the sun; and he cried with a loud voice, saying, to all the fowls that fly in the midst of heaven, Come and gather yourselves together unto the supper of the great God;

¹⁸That ye may eat the flesh of kings, and the flesh of captains, and the flesh of mighty men, and the flesh of horses, and of them that sit on them, and the flesh of all men, both free and bond, both small and great.

¹⁹And I saw the beast, and the kings of the earth, and their armies, gathered together to make war against him that sat on the horse, and against his army.

²⁰And the beast was taken, and with him the false prophet that wrought miracles before him, with which he deceived

them that had received the mark of the beast, and them that worshipped his image. These both were cast alive into a lake of fire burning with brimstone.

[21]And the remnant were slain with the sword of him that sat upon the horse, which sword proceeded out of his mouth: and all the fowls were filled with their flesh.

CHAPTER TEN

WHY?

What was it that brought all these armies to this small, rather insignificant section of the earth's crust? For years I wrestled with this question. The battle of Armageddon didn't make sense. Why would the armies of the world be at that place, at that time, for that purpose? It seemed to be the wrong war, at the wrong time, for the wrong reason, at the wrong place.

In the natural realm it was. But God - He brings together all things to fulfill his supernatural promises, and involves natural conditions and situations. God knew at the beginning of days, alpha days, what would transpire at the end of days, omega days. He is the alpha and the omega. He is the beginner and the ender.

> Alpha is the first letter of the Greek alphabet; Omega is the last. Alpha and Omega symbolize the beginning and the end. Revelation 1:8 states, "'I am the Alpha and the Omega,' says the Lord God, who is, and who w as, and who is to come, the Almighty.'" (NIV)

He is the author and the finisher. He knew. He knew that man would eventually develop a technology that would require a gigantically perverse amount of energy to fuel it. He knew that oil would become the favorite fuel of "latter day" nations. He knew that the military and industrial might of each country would be dependent on each country's possession of oil.

He knew that during the oil glut of the 1950's and 1960's man would squander a great portion of that earth honey. He knew that the Arab-Israeli war of 1973 would trigger the energy crisis, the petroleum polarization of the international body politic, and the greatest transfer of wealth in history. He knew that by 1980 all industrial nations would be near hysteria, first for lack of oil, and then for the extortionary price of it. Even though the 1980's and 1990's would see frantic oil exploration and discovery in the world, the problem had not been abated.

Much oil is now being pumped from new non-traditional fields, but I think that this only exacerbates the situation. It serves to have polarized the problems, rather than solved them. The price of petroleum is still very high, and at the first sign of international crisis triggered by terrorism or regional wars, could skyrocket to stratospheric heights. Yet, even this temporary semi-reprieve in supply and demand was foreknown.

> We know only too well that the polarization of countries, political factions, economies, and ideologies over oil is far more relevant today than when these words were first penned. The price of crude oil hit an all time high in 2007.

God Had a Foreknowledge of All Things

The foreknowledge of God about hidden petroleum was just a part of his knowing before. His purposes and subsequent design for natural man's creation and ultimate spiritual relationship was in his mind long before man's earthly kingdom was begun.

From man's Edenic beginning he has foundered and fumbled in his half-hearted attempts to add God to his human kingdom. Man rarely realized that God's kingdom was present and operating successfully long before the kingdom of man was born. It was, as we all know, the kingdom of man that was added to the kingdom of God.

Coming forth from the mind of God in the extended establishment of his kingdom on earth was a prophetic poem, woven into a scriptural tapestry that will someday hang on the walls of eternity. The temporal and unimportant social designation of "Jew" and "Gentile" has no place on those eternal walls. They are both appellations by men and for men, used divisively to separate man from man and man from God. In that "great day coming" we will have new names "And the Gentiles shall see thy righteousness, and all kings thy glory: and thou shalt be called by a new name, which the mouth of the Lord shall name" (Isaiah 62:2). That unity that we have longed for will finally be ours, even as Jesus prayed that it would be:

> That they all may be one; as thou, Father, art in me, and I
> in thee, that they also may be one in us: that the world
> may believe that thou hast sent me.
>
> John 17:21

Temporal Israel is Not Eternal Israel

If the earthly, human designation of *"Jew"* and *"Gentile"* will be subsumed in glory, how about that mighty but mysterious name *"Israel"*? We have already learned that there are seven *"Israels"* that exist biblically and contemporarily.

For a free downloadable copy of Jim Spillman's The Seven Israels go to *www.JimSpillmanMinistries.org*.

Are any of these eternal in nature, or are they all just temporal? It is easily understood that the seventh Israel, the modern state of Israel, even as Germany and England, has no heavenly meaning or place. Israel is an earthly nation couched in earthly history. It is not an entity to be considered in the "new heaven and the new earth": "And I saw a new heaven and a new earth: for the first heaven and the first earth were passed away; and there was no more sea" (Revelation 21:1).

What of Biblical Israel, of Jacob, the children of Israel coming into Canaan, the Northern Kingdom, and the Babylon returnees? These four Israels are the historic narrative of God's plan to begin the physical counterpart in the presentation of His true, eternal Israel. Again, they were temporal designations standing for the earthly initiation and development of God's redemptive plan. They are not to be exhumed and synthetically restored for life and practice in God's earthly community today. These last days were never meant to be a reprise of the times of the law or practice of the people of the law. Hebrews 7:19 declares: "For the law made nothing perfect, but the bringing in of a better hope did; by the which we draw nigh unto God."

The New Israel Relationship

The writer of Hebrews goes on in chapter 8, to discuss their "new" Israel relationship in a highly definitive way:

> [1]Now of the things which we have spoken this is the sum: We have such an high priest, who is set on the right hand of the throne of the Majesty in the heavens;

> [2]A minister of the sanctuary, and of the true tabernacle, which the Lord pitched, and not man.

> [4]For if he were on earth, he should not be a priest, seeing that there are priests that offer gifts according to the law:

> [5]Who serve unto the example and shadow of heavenly things....

> [6]But now hath he obtained a more excellent ministry, by how much also he is the mediator of a better covenant, which was established upon better promises.

[7]For if that first covenant had been faultless, then should no place have been sought for the second.

[8]For finding fault with them, he saith, Behold, the days come, saith the Lord, when I will make a new covenant with the house of Israel and with the house of Judah:

[9]Not according to the covenant that I made with their fathers in the day when I took them by the hand to lead them out of the land of Egypt; because they continued not in my covenant, and I regarded them not, saith the Lord.

[10]For this is the covenant that I will make with the house of Israel after those days, saith the Lord; I will put my laws into their mind, and write them in their hearts: and I will be to them a God, and they shall be to me a people:

[12]For I will be merciful to their unrighteousness, and their sins and their iniquities will I remember no more.

[13]In that he saith, A new covenant, he hath made the first old. Now that which decayeth and waxeth old is ready to vanish away.

A Final Word on the Land

This brings us to the consideration of the fifth Israel, the land. Even though the historic, biblical people of Israel lived on the land called "Canaan" and then called "Israel" this land had a purpose and a place in God's plan that went beyond the history of Bible people. The land was formed, designated and enriched long before Jacob was a prophetic personality. The land came before the people. The land not only has a past, but it has a millennial future. It will play a part in the plan of God until it is replaced by the "new earth" (Revelation 21:1).

> Israel will be known as "the camp of God's people," with Jerusalem "the city he loves" as its capital (Revelation 20:9) for a thousand years before God's final judgment and the establishment of a "new earth".

The "Israel of God"

We must finally remember the "Israel of God" of Galatians 6:16. This Israel is the "household of faith" established in Christ Jesus. This Israel is the figure of which the other personal Israels were "shadows" (Hebrews 8:5). It was conceived in the foreknowledge of God (Romans 8:29), and consummated in the spiritual lives of men (Corinthians 3:16, 17).

All of these things that we have studied in this book find their place in the Kingdom of God of which Jesus spoke: "And I appoint unto you a kingdom, as my Father hath appointed unto me" (Luke 22:29). The entrance into this kingdom is through the new birth of which Jesus spoke: "Jesus answered and said unto him, Verily, verily, I say unto thee, Except a man be born again, he cannot see the kingdom of God" (John 3:3)

To learn more about this "New Birth" see Appendix A "Spiritual Help"

Paul, in Colossians explained it so very well:

[13]Who hath delivered us from the power of darkness, and hath translated us into the kingdom of his dear Son:

[14]In whom we have redemption through his blood, even the forgiveness of sins:

[15]Who is the image of the invisible God, the firstborn of every creature:

[16]For by him were all things created, that are in heaven, and that are in earth, visible and invisible, whether they be thrones, or dominions, or principalities, or powers: all things were created by him, and for him:

[17]And he is before all things, and by him all things consist.

¹⁸And he is the head of the body, the church: who is the beginning, the firstborn from the dead; that in all things he might have the pre-eminence.

¹⁹For it pleased the Father that in him should all fulness dwell;

Colossians 1:13-19

The Tapestry of the Kingdom

We conclude, thankfully, that indeed "all fullness" shall "dwell" in Him. The multi-colored threads spun before Eden's arboretum have even now been woven into the tapestry of the kingdom story. From the black thread of buried treasure, to the bright blue of prophecy's promises, to the purples and browns of historic Israel, to the living vibrant gold of the "Israel of God," intertwined with the blood red thread of redemption's life line, the tapestry hangs before us.

Breaking the Treasure Code

The Hunt For
Israel's Oil

Book II

CHAPTER ELEVEN

THE SEARCH

There's an old joke in Israel. *Moses wandered the desert for forty years and settled in the only spot in the Middle East that had no oil.* The joke has become the stinging epithet of Israel's search for oil within its borders.

Beginnings

Limited exploration in Palestine from 1900 until 1948 turned up little but the belief that oil may lie somewhere in the south; possibly beneath the Dead Sea or the Northern Negev desert. European nations, attracted to the Middle East's oil potential, spent the last part of the nineteenth and first part of the twentieth centuries tussling over territories in the region. They divvyed up land according to their national power to hold onto it and each countries economic interests.

The British controlled Palestine and a good bit of the rest of the Middle East during this period. Oil exploration contracts were issued and controlled under their mandate. IPC (Iraqi Petroleum Company), a British controlled European consortium including BP (British Petroleum), Shell (Anglo/Dutch), Elf (French), Exxon and Mobil, showed interest in the Heletz area of southern Palestine; a part of the northern Negev desert.

IPC drilled the first oil exploration well in Palestine, dubbed Hulikhat, in 1947. Political violence in the area was beginning to erupt due to Israel's upcoming independence date, forcing IPC to stop drilling before their target depth was reached.

In the 1930's IPC was also responsible for the construction of an oil pipeline from the Kirkuk oilfields in northern Iraq to the seaport of Haifa in Palestine. At that time the Middle East was under either British or French influence. The idea of an oil pipeline from Iraq to the Mediterranean port in Haifa, seemed like a safe, economic method for transporting oil to waiting tankers. IPC's British owners never imagined in 1930 that the creation of independent Arab and Jewish states in Palestine after World War II would forever preclude Arab oil flowing through Jewish Israel to Haifa.

Arab oil flowing to world markets through Israel is not an alternative open for discussion among Israel's neighbors. The pipeline still exists, but as long as the Arab nations have anything to say about it, no oil will ever flow from Kirkuk to Haifa.

Independence

Israel became an independent state on May 14, 1948 and immediately cancelled all existing oil licenses granted under British Mandate.

Israel's Arab neighbor enemies, now independent states themselves, vowed to push her into the sea on the day she was born. The moment the British authority pulled out of the Israel. they acted to make good on their vow.

Israel, however, was not pushed into the sea by her enemies. Every time Arab nations attacked, Israel rebuffed, taking more territory with each enemy "advance."

Her enemies were beaten back for the time being and once Israel's prognosis for survival as a nation moved from *critical* to *guarded*, Israelis turned their attention to building a national infrastructure. One of the foundations of any national infrastructure is energy and one of the primary sources of energy is oil. By 1952 the Israeli Petroleum Law was enacted.

The Israeli Petroleum Law

The Israeli Petroleum Law states that "petroleum resources belong to the State." These State owned resources extend beyond the land itself to include Israel's territorial waters.

The Law governs all exploration and production of all petroleum products. It provides three types of permits to explore for or produce petroleum in the country. The first "preliminary permit" allows the holder to conduct initial prospecting in the permit area with the exception of drilling. This eighteen month permit also gives the holder the privilege of requesting a "priority right" on the permit area. The priority right prevents awarding the area's petroleum rights to anyone else during the term of the permit. The second permit stage is a three to four year "exploration license." This license allows the drilling of test wells in an area of not more than 400,000 dunam (100,000 acres). If and when a prospector discovers oil in economically retrievable quantities under the exploration license he may apply for a "production lease." The production lease term is thirty years, extendable to fifty years.

Just because a company has been granted an exploration or production license in an area doesn't mean it is granted physical access to the area. Once issued a permit, license, or lease, the holder must also secure permission from other State agencies and property owners to actually conduct activities in the license area. The holder is also required to submit regular progress reports and final reports to Ministry of Infrastructure. All research, test results, studies and any other information produced through exploration efforts are to be submitted to the Ministry as the property of the state.

The production lease gives the lessee the right to market any petroleum produced, subject to the State of Israel preempting the petroleum for its own use. Israel also collects a 12½% royalty on all petroleum produced. All in all, Israel's petroleum law effectively allows outside commercial entities (the licensees) to finance the exploration and production of oil in the country. Israel benefits by having access to all the exploration data and 12 ½% of all the oil produced.

Drilling

In 1955 the Hulikhat well, Israel's first ever, was reopened and Israel was in the oil business. Hulikhat produced a steady, but modest flow of oil and became the premier well in what came to be known as the "Heletz Oil Field Discovery." The Heletz field has produced 18 million barrels of oil (virtually all of Israel's domestic production) since its opening in 1955. The field is still in production today but the flow is now a trickle and its reserves are nearly exhausted.

The country's next big energy find was the Zohar gas field, also in the northern Negev; just a stone's throw from Heletz. The Zohar gas field has produced 30 billion cubic feet of gas to date but it too is showing signs of old age. Heletz and Zohar production were never world class and today, production is marginal at best.

As the new millennium dawned a surprise discovery brightened Israel's energy future. Natural gas, and plenty of it, was discovered off the coast of Ashkelon and Gaza. The offshore gas field's estimated reserves at 3.5 trillion cubic feet are a boon to Israel's energy future. Today Israel's domestic natural gas is slated to replace oil as fuel for the country's electrical generating stations.

Israel was lucky early on with the Heletz and Zohar discoveries. The recent offshore gas field discovery provides the fuel needed for much of the country's electrical power, but new petroleum discoveries have been virtually non-existent. If Israel had oil under its surface, as a lot of folks believed she did, they sure were having difficulty finding it.

The northern Negev had always been a focal point for Israeli oil and gas exploration because of the early wins with Heletz and Zohar. Maybe it was time to look elsewhere.

The Dead Sea

The Dead Sea region was another area of early oil exploration interest. As far back as written records go, historical mention of tar pits in the Dead Sea area is common. Genesis 14:10 states:

> Now the Valley of Siddim was full of tar pits, and when the kings of Sodom and Gomorrah fled, some of the men fell into them and the rest fled to the hills.

The Greek geographer, Strabo (63 BC–21 AD) noted that:

> Near the area of Masada, liquid pitch could be observed dropping out of the rocks. Vapours arose from the Dead Sea, itself, that ignited very easily. Sodom and Gomorrah being destroyed by fire; fires are seen in the area. This country is full of fire.

The Dead Sea had always been considered rich in minerals and with all of the historical references to open tar pits it seemed like an ideal place to look for oil. Petroleum prospectors figured that where there's pitch, there's oil. Until very recently, the connection had yet to prove any marketable results.

The Dead Sea was believed by some evangelical Christian oil men to be one of God's favorite spots. One of the more flamboyant evangelicals, a ten gallon hat wearing Texas

111

oil man on a mission to "discover oil for God and Israel" got a lot of press but came up short of actually finding petroleum.

No matter who the players were, it seemed that the Dead Sea gamble came up dry for everyone. In the last of a series of articles about a major Dead Sea oil exploration effort in the early 1990's, Israel Business Today gave a brief summary of the hunt for Dead Sea oil.

> The oil exploration project at the Sdom Amok 1 drill site near the Dead Sea has been suspended following no signs of oil...The Sdom Amok project is the deepest and most expensive oil drill ever conducted in Israel. The companies involved have spent $20 million on the drilling and another $3 million on production tests. Drills have been conducted to a maximum depth of 6.4 km and could be extended as deep as 7.5 km. According to published reports, the drilling equipment which has been at Sdom Amok since the beginning of 1992 will be dismantled and reassembled at a site in the Besor region of the northwestern Negev...[1]

It seemed that everyone had given up on looking for oil near the Dead Sea. But then something happened that may have sparked Dead Sea exploration back to life. Israel's Genco Corporation made a *small* discovery near the Dead Sea in 2006. Small in oil reserves terms is still big in human terms. Genco's small discovery was estimated at between four and six million barrels and worth about $300 million!

The Bible Prospectors

Israel's early focus on oil exploration had always been in the south. The Negev and Dead Sea kept the attention of Israel's oil prospectors. The country's northern territories were outside of the spotlight of official attention, but the north

---

[1] Back to proven territory in the Northern Negev

country was the center of focus for a different group of *oil hunters*. This group was different in that their information came from a unique source. The *data* and *maps* used by oil hunters in the north came from the pages of the Bible.

Specifically citing passages in Genesis and Deuteronomy, they understood phrases like "... Out of Asher his bread shall be fat ..."; "... blessings of the deep that lieth under ..." and "... let him dip his foot in oil ..." to mean that God had promised the children of Israel a vast treasure of oil and provided clues as to where it was located. The oil, according to these Bible based hunters, was beneath specific tribal territories of Jacob's children.

Asher's Oil

Wesley Hancock discovered that he was Jewish on a train in 1941. He was getting married and for the first time in his life he looked at his birth certificate. His mother's maiden name was Goldstein. What a shock! His mother's family had immigrated to the United States from Bucharest, Romania when she was only three. Apparently the family was afraid that the stigma of being Jewish would hold them back in their new country. The fear was passed on to the next generation and Wesley's mother hid their Jewish roots from her children. It shocked and scandalized the other children, but not Wes. Wes had become a born-again Christian in his youth and this new *relationship* to his Savior fascinated him.

A newspaper clipping Wes happened on in 1958 stirred something in him. The clipping told of a pastor Herman Walters of the Foursquare Gospel Church delivering a sermon about Israel, preaching that God told Moses he would find oil in Palestine. The preacher used Deuteronomy 33:19 as his reference, speaking of Zebulun and Issachar "... suck[ing] of the abundance of the seas, and of treasures hid in the sand."

Wes, like those who were to come after him, was captivated. As he studied scripture, the name of Asher continually came to his mind. He adopted as his mantra the passage, also in Deuteronomy 33, referring to Asher "... dip[ping] his foot in oil."

Wes showed up in Israel in November of 1959 to meet with Israeli Oil Commissioner Peretz Grader. Grader told Hancock that no exploration licenses were available, but to come back in a year or so and check again. Wesley took Grader's rejection as a firm appointment.

By 1961 Hancock was awarded an exploration license of 392,000 dunam (97,000 acres) north and east of Mount Carmel near Haifa. The license area included Mount Carmel and extended into parts of the Jezreel Valley, known as the "Valley of Megiddo," site of the prophesied last day battle of Armageddon.

Armed with a report forecasting Israel's oil potential, and his *Asher* passage, Wesley went looking for Asher's oil.

On September 19, 1963 Wesley spudded the Asher #1 in northern Israel. Asher #1 was drilled to a depth of 7,800 feet when the drill head twisted off, taking seven drill collars with it. After the *twistoff,* chances of drilling any deeper were nil. By January of 1964, testing in the hole above 7,800 feet revealed that the Asher #1 was dry.

In 1965 Wesley commissioned a hydrocarbon survey of his license area. This was the first petroleum survey of its kind in Northern Israel. The survey results led to choosing his location for the Asher #2 well. Hancock drilled the Asher #2 to a depth of 4,300 feet and core samples showed traces of oil. The Asher #2, however, had to be shut down.

Wesley Hancock had run out of money. Wes didn't have any outside investors; the money he spent was his own and he spent all of it. Nine hundred thousand dollars in 1960 was worth what $6 million is today. It was Wesley's fortune and he spent it. More than forty years later Wes doesn't regret a bit of it. There is still excitement in his voice when he speaks about Asher's oil.

Gilman Hill

In 1979 Gilman Hill, another American evangelical Christian, came to Israel looking for Asher's oil. Unlike other Christian oil hunters, Gilman didn't rely on Old Testament passages or tribal maps to locate a well site. According to Hill, God directed him to drill for oil and showed him the well's location during a 1978 tour of Mount Carmel.

Sponsored by Utah's Mount Carmel Trust, Gill had completed preliminary geological surveys and fulfilled permit requirements to begin drilling by 1980.

The government of Israel is always interested about where the money to fund foreign oil prospectors comes from. In Gilman Hill's case, they were very interested in just who was behind the Mount Carmel Trust.

Interviewing Gillman on the subject, then Israeli Energy Minister Moday wanted to know specifically, just who was behind the Trust. "Is there Israeli money involved in this project?" Moday asked.

"No," was Hills response.

"Is there American Jewish money involved in this project?" inquired Moday. Again, Hill's reply was negative. Growing impatient, Moday asked finally, "Are American Christians funding this project?"

Gilman's response again was, "No." Frustrating Moday further, Gilman offered a cryptic explanation, "The Trust has two partners. I am a one percent partner, my associate is a ninety-nine percent partner. I have no financial ownership in the Trust, it is funded completely by my partner.

I do, however, speak and act on his behalf and I have complete power of attorney for the Trust."

Impressed but not more informed, Moday continued, "Can you arrange for me to meet your partner?"

"I would be delighted to introduce you to him," Gilman replied. "My partner is the God of Abraham, Isaac, and Jacob; I am sure he would be very interested in you meeting him."

Realizing that he had been bested and would get no further on the subject, he completed the interview, "Mr. Hill, you are a Christian and I am a Jew; but everyday I will pray for your success with this project."

Shaking hands with Moday as he was leaving Hill offered Moday a final reply, "Mr. Moday, you are a Jew and I am a Christian; but every day I will pray for you and for your success in the position God has placed you." From that point forward Hill's relationship with the State of Israel and with Energy Minister Moday was secure.

Gilman Hill's well, Elijah I, was to be drilled to the upper Triassic strata, a depth of 15,000 to 16,000 feet. At 8,900 feet Gilman halted the drilling. According to Hill, God had told him to stop. Receiving the Divine message, "circumstances have changed," Gil was convinced that he was to cease drilling until further notice from God. Frustrated that he was first led by God to begin drilling in Israel, then led to stop drilling without explanation. Gil continued his geologic research for another six years waiting for the Divine release to resume drilling. The release never came.

Gil continued working in Israel while he waited; adding to his geologic research. During his time in Israel he began a successful prison ministry and proposed a water resource program that would supply southern Lebanon and northern Israel with sufficient water to ensure long term agricultural prosperity. The Elijah 1 well, however, was never to be reopened. After spending $6 million of his own money on Mount Carmel, drawn by the Bible's promise that Asher would "dip his foot in oil," he had failed to find the elusive flow. To his credit, Gil quietly paid all of the debts associated with his project and went home. Today, in Israel, when the subject of American Christians and oil comes up, Gilman Hill is remembered honorably.

Andy SoRelle

About the same time Hill started drilling Elijah 1, a Texas oil man named Andy SoRelle was busy preparing the Atlit 1 well near Haifa, known as the Asher Project. SoRelle first visited Israel in 1968 as part of a thirteen nation tour.

As is common with Christian pilgrims to the Holy Land, Andy developed a connection with the land and people of Israel. Being an evangelical Christian, he was interested in the spiritual and political future of Israel. As an oil man, his visit also birthed a concern in his heart for the problem of Israel's oil future. He wondered at the seeming lack of oil exploration efforts in the country. The Heletz field in the Negev was active, but it consisted of shallow sand wells. He couldn't believe Heletz was a substantial long term answer to Israel's oil supply. Andy returned home from his 1968 tour with the seed of Israel and its oil future planted in his soul.

His next opportunity to do something about Israel's oil future came in 1976. Energy Exploration, Inc., SoRelle's Houston based company, had just developed a new technology for detecting petroleum deposits. "Radio Metrics" measured isotopic emissions radiating from potential petroleum deposits.

SoRelle wrote to the Israeli government, offering to prospect in Israel, at his own expense, using his new technology. After month's had passed and frustrated by the skepticism and lack of response from Israel, SoRelle drafted a harshly worded letter to the Israeli government regarding their failure to accept an offer of free services to their benefit. Apparently the strong sentiments got their attention. Israel sent an oil expert to Houston to determine SoRelle's validity and check out his new technology.

Two weeks after the Israeli's visit, SoRelle was invited to prospect for oil in Israel. In the autumn of 1977 Andy returned to Israel with his Radio Metric equipment. After poor showings at several INOC (Israel National Oil Company) sites, Andy moved his equipment, at the government's request, to the Sinai. Within a few weeks, using his Radio Metric equipment, he found a site with high probability of oil.

Andy immediately applied for an exploration permit in the Sinai. Unfortunately, at the same time Anwar Sadat of Egypt was traveling to Jerusalem in hope of regaining the Sinai from Israel, who had taken the land from Egypt during the 1973 Yom Kippur War. Peace talks put further oil exploration in the area on hold. Andy was stuck on hold for two years while Egypt and Israel worked through a peace plan. In March of 1979 the Israel-Egypt Peace Treaty was signed as the first realization of the 1978 Camp David Peace Accords. Provisions in the treaty called for Israel to return possession of the Sinai to Egypt. Andy SoRelle's plans for drilling in the Sinai went from "on-hold" to non-existent.

Undaunted, Andy discovered another approach to finding oil in Israel. Using Deuteronomy 32:24 and a Bible map of Israel's ancient tribal lands as his guides he returned to Israel to find the oil the Bible had promised in the "foot of Asher."

Speaking with Israel's chief geologist, he learned that the ancient tribal land of Asher, the area between Haifa and Caesarea, was the only part of Israel that hadn't been surveyed by oil explorers. Andy applied for, and was granted a 100,000 acre exploration license, "block 174 Carmel Coast", named "The Asher Project" by SoRelle.

Andy SoRelle's first and only well, the Atlit1, was spudded in February 1981, the same year Jim Spillman's original book about Israel's oil, *The Great Treasure Hunt*, was released. Spillman and SoRelle were mutual supporters, each understandably interested in the work of the other. Throughout SoRelle's career in Israel he updated Spillman on the progress of the well they both believed would strike the oil God had promised to Jacob's children nearly 4,000 years earlier.

The Atlit 1 well, located just inside Israel's Atlit Naval Base and adjacent to the ruins of a crusader castle was plagued with drilling problems from its beginning. Clearing the drill rig site, a bulldozer uncovered rooftops from an ancient crusader city believed to have been built the same time as the castle. Additionally, archaeologists discovered that the crusader city had been built on top of an earlier Phoenician city. Atlit 1 became an historical treasure overnight.

In order to preserve any ancient artifacts directly below the drilling area SoRelle and Israel's Antiquities Ministry came to a compromise. Rather than grade the site for the drill rig, Andy agreed to fill the drill site, therefore preserving any artifacts that may lie beneath the existing grade of the land. This compromise cost SoRelle an additional $60,000.

The drill rig, an Ideco Super 7-11, was rated to a depth of 15,000 feet. At 9,400 feet the dill bit hit volcanic rock. Volcanic flows of 700 to 1,000 feet thick were a common occurrence, so hitting this stratum didn't surprise anyone. Their surprise came as they drilled continually deeper, without breaking out of the volcanic layer. They drilled down through another 7600 feet of volcanic rock before finally coming into limestone again. The Ideco drill rig now at 17,296 feet was way beyond its capacity. Fearing he would lose the hole and the rig, Atlit's drilling supervisor, Vic Lambert, shut down the operation until a larger rig could be brought in.

December 28, 1982, more than a year after the drilling at Atlit I had been suspended, the new Lapidoth Emsco 1500 drill rig, rated at 26,000 feet was installed over the original hole. This new phase, dubbed the Atlit II was planned to bring the well as deep as 23,000 feet. By February of 1983 the well had been cleaned out and depth had been increased to 18,000 feet.

Drilling continued without incident until, at 20,570 feet Atlit II struck oil! What oil experts call "very good shows" came to the surface; graded as light oil at 35 to 40 degrees API; very good stuff! SoRelle continued to a final depth of 21,431 feet. The "pay zone," the zone of oil bearing rock, was estimated at 470 feet, from 20,570 to 21,309 feet. The drilling of Atlit II was finally complete! Now it was time to develop the well.

During the development phase problems emerged again. Financing for the project had been shoe-string at best for quite some time. The crew had stopped casing the well at 13,772 feet. Casing is the steel sleeve installed as the hole is drilled, to keep it from caving in on itself.

Atlit I was cased with 13 3/8 inch steel casing to 2,742 feet, then a smaller 9 5/8 inch casing to 4,643 feet, finally a 7 inch casing to 13,732 feet. After 13,732 feet the casing stopped. Not having funds for additional casing and reasoning that the volcanic rock they had struggled through was stable enough to hold the hole open the crew continued drilling in "open hole," without casing.

"Drilling Magazine," in its October 1984 issue describes the heartbreaking events that happened during the development phase.

> The decision was made to go for a completion which included setting a 5-in. liner in the open hole section and perforating the pay zone. Special 5-in. pipe was shipped to Haifa, and the crew was cleaning the hole in preparation when more trouble struck. Tripping out, the

drill collars stuck at 18,669 ft and two weeks of jarring would not break them loose. Special equipment was flown in from the U.S. to retrieve the fish (130 ft. in length) and, while cleaning the hole to "fish" with the new equipment they stuck again at the 17,772 ft mark. After ten more days of trying to break loose, they came out leaving another 8 ½ ft fish in the hole.

August 24, 1983, more than two and a half years after spudding, Andy SoRelle called it quits for the Atlit hole. At $20,000 a day in drilling expenses, the money had run out and after two instances of catastrophic bad luck the hole was permanently closed. Having spent more than $25 million, his own money and that of his investors, Andy gave up on the hole, But he never surrendered his dream of discovering Asher's oil.

Andy SoRelle was out of money and, at sixty-four, he felt the project had also taken its toll on him personally. Atlit I and Atlit II had spent more than his money. The last three years had exhausted him physically as well.

His indomitable spirit, however, was still intact. SoRelle did what most wildcat oil men do when faced with irrecoverable losses and shattering disappointment, he began planning for a new drill site, the Atlit III.

Andy returned to the States to raise money for Atlit III but funding proved elusive. His investors, oil men, business professionals and church groups, had trusted him with money for Atlit I and Atlit II. Why should they think he wouldn't come up dry on Atlit III as well? "God may have promised oil to Israel's children," they reasoned, "but was Andy the man God had chosen to deliver it?"

Lack of money, Andy's poor health, and growing Palestinian violence have all been cited as reasons for the still birth of Atlit III. Whatever the reasons, the time and individual had not yet arrived to discover of oil in Israel.

Tovia Luskin

In a story that seems to be dominated by Christian oil explorers, it's a little ironic that the only oilman, using the same scriptures as the Christian explorers, to actually have discovered oil in Israel, is Jewish.

Tovia Luskin, like his evangelical Christian American counterparts, has been searching for oil in Israel for a long time now - nineteen years. Like his evangelical Christian American counterparts, Tovia used the Bible as his guide for finding oil in the Holy Land. Unlike his evangelical Christian American counterparts, Tovia is a Jew. Also, unlike his evangelical American Christian counterparts, he has actually discovered the oil promised to the Children of Israel in Genesis and Deuteronomy!

Luskin, a Russian Jew and a geologist, earned degrees in geophysics at Moscow State University. As a former lead geologist for Shell Oil and advisor to Bridge Oil in Sydney, Australia, his extensive background in the oil industry gave him the professional credence to back up his religious conviction that there was indeed, oil in Israel.

Working in Australia in 1988, Tovia, new as a practicing Jew, came upon a passage in the Torah in Deuteronomy.

Tovia is naturally quiet about sharing his religious beliefs concerning the oil with skeptics who would use them to discount his professional and technical efforts on the project. But to those sincerely interested, he happily quotes from memory the passage that began his quest:

> About Joseph, he (Moses) said: "May the Lord bless his land with the precious dew from heaven above and the deep waters that lie below; with the best the sun brings forth and the finest the moon can yield; with the choicest gifts of the ancient mountains and the fruitfulness of the everlasting hills…"

> (Deut. 33:13 NIV)

This passage in Deuteronomy along with his discovery that the medieval Jewish scholar Rashi interpreted the passage to mean that the "everlasting hills" were much older than the surrounding countryside was proof that he was on to something.

Rashi's interpretation struck home with Luskin. He knew, as a geologist, that the concept of one geological feature (the hills) being of a different age than the land surrounding it was an accepted fundamental of modern geological science. But this concept was unknown in the time Rashi wrote his interpretation. In Luskin's view, Rashi had no way of interpreting the passage this way other than by divine guidance.

These two proofs were enough for him to write to Rebbe Menachem Mendel Schneerson, one of the world's renowned Jewish scholars, for his review and consideration of the interpretations. After reviewing his material, the Rebbe, responded noting, "I had pleasure in reading your discussion ..." and "... You will tell me good news ...."

This was enough for Luskin to get serious about taking action. He traveled to New York for a personal audience with the Rebbe. The Rebbe pronounced over him a Bracha (blessing) regarding his proposed search for oil in the Promised Land, "You have my blessing that you will have good news in the near future." This innocuous sounding blessing carried tremendous authority for Luskin. He believed the Rebbe to be G_d's Moshiach (Messiah), the one to bring redemption to the Jews. This was enough for Luskin to sell his home in Sydney, Australia and immigrate to Israel.

By 1993 Tovia Luskin had assembled an impressive team of geologists and oil experts (most of them Russian from his previous acquaintance at Moscow Sate University) to form Givot Olam Oil Exploration, LLC. Givot Olam, Hebrew for "everlasting hills," secured a 62,500 acre exploration license just north and east of Tel Aviv.

Their first well, the Meged 2, was drilled in 1994 and successfully tested 40° API oil at 17,000 feet. In 1998 the Meged 2 was retested and showed a 400 barrel per day flow rate. The Meged 3 well was drilled two years later a few miles to the west of the Meged 2. This well logged 47 feet of pay (the vertical area of the well from which to extract oil) at 15,000 feet deep, but had to be shut down because of mechanical problems in the hole. The Meged 4, north of the Meged 2 and Meged 3, was drilled in 2003. At 16,000 feet the Meged 4 began flowing oil and gas. The rate of flow was unspecified but Givot Olam reported a commercial discovery of 980 million barrels. With the Meged 4 discovery the Givot Olam eighteen month exploration license became a thirty year production lease.

Today Givot Olam is in the process of developing the Meged Oil Field with plans for 10 wells in a 50 square kilometer project area. With proper development each well is conservatively estimated to produce over 900 barrels per day for the first year, and then decline to a steady 400 barrels per day over each well's seven year expected lifespan. The ten wells in this field, roughly one-fifth of Givot Olam's production lease area, in the conservative view is capable of producing over 12 million barrels of oil over the next seven years.

Israel has only produced 20 million barrels in its entire fifty year history of oil production. Personally Luskin estimates the Givot Olam lease area to hold as many as a billion barrels of oil. Twenty percent of those billion barrels, Luskin believes, is recoverable. Two hundred million barrels at $70.00 or more a barrel adds up to fourteen billion dollars. Not bad for Jewish Russian immigrant using the Torah and his Rebbe's blessing as a guide!

CHAPTER TWELVE

JOHN BROWN

John Brown is a man of faith; he takes God at his word … literally. But he wasn't always that way. In 1981 John was a fast track executive in a rapidly growing Michigan cutting tool company. A world of non-stop work, private jets, plenty of money, and free flowing booze brought John's life to a crisis point. The pace, the money and the booze were taking its toll.

Troubled over his rip-tear lifestyle and increasing alcoholism, John's wife and business partners pushed him to get help. But stints in alcohol treatment centers didn't seem to have any lasting effect.

Then something happened. Help came from a direction no one around him expected. John's family and colleagues considered his alcoholism a crisis; but for them the real disaster came when he found the cure.

John Brown met God. His conversion manifested itself in an instant and polar change. One day he was non-stop, hell-bent, heavy drinking John Brown. The next he had completely lost his taste for booze and the wild life. The alcoholic in John was gone; as if it had never existed.

Before John met God and accepted His Son Jesus Christ as savior his partners were worried and his wife was fed up. He was a pain, but at least it was a pain they recognized. After John committed his life to serving God, he became a man his wife and colleagues didn't recognize; and it troubled them more.

The new John had no taste for booze; seemingly cured instantly of his alcoholism. In their eyes, that was a good thing. But there was something they weren't so comfortable with. John had become a believer - a born again, dyed in the wool, utterly shameless, really fanatical, true believer.

He witnessed to everyone - everywhere! He told them how God had saved him, delivered him from alcoholism, brought hope and joy into his life. At work he told everyone in his path about Jesus. Handing out cards that said, *"JESUS LOVES YOU"* on the front, with instructions for *"How to Make Heaven Your Home"* on the back.

John asked people if they were saved; if the answer was no, he'd ask, did they want to be! His colleagues didn't know what to do with him. In the business, the old John was a guy to be watched out for; now the new John was becoming the guy to be avoided.

A Crisis at Home

If the reception at work was bad; the one at home was worse. John's wife definitely saw the change and she just couldn't reconcile herself with the new man. Yesterday she was sure that her husband would drink or work himself to death. Today she had a religious fanatic to deal with.

She couldn't cope with this new man and his message of Jesus, and love, and salvation. John's behavior scared her more now than when he was drinking! She didn't know the solution, but the problem seemed to be a religious one. It was time to get the Church involved.

The Browns were Catholic. John wasn't much for attending mass, but the family *was* baptized into the Church. An appointment was made with the parish priest.

Alcoholism and marriage problems were common topics for parishioners to seek counsel on. Religious fanaticism was less common. In the eyes of the Church, one of the problems with new converts, especially *true believers* like John was that they lacked the restraint those fortunate enough to have been born into the Church benefit from.

When the Browns met with their parish priest John asked him the same question he asked everyone he met; did he know Jesus? The reaction wasn't pleasant. Did the priest know Jesus?! Did he know Jesus?! He was a priest for crying out loud! He was the man the Church had assigned as a shepherd to this flock. Now one of the flock had the gall to ask if he knew Jesus?!

Annulment

The priest's assessment was quick and to the point. Here was a man who barely attended mass, knew little about the workings and hierarchy of the Church, and had the nerve to ask if his priest knew Jesus. This new convert, *probably protestant,* was obviously overcome by religious zeal, unwilling to listen to reason, and unwilling to accept the priest's authority as his appointed spiritual leader. This was a problematic and potentially dangerous situation.

If left to pursue his course of unrestrained evangelism, this man could damage the circumspect reputation of the parish and subsequently destroy his family's standing in the Church. The priest's decision was harsh, but for the sake of the parish, the eternal security of his family and the safety of the Kingdom in general, drastic action had to be taken.

With John's wife's permission, the priest arranged for a religious annulment. In the eyes of the Church, John Brown no longer had a wife or children. As far as the Catholic Church was concerned, John Brown no longer existed. He was excommunicated. In the stroke of a pen this new convert, this man who had just met Jesus face to face, lost his family and his church.

Jacob's Blessing

John Brown, however, was a true believer. He knew what he knew. Meeting God was real. It was the most real thing that had ever happened to him. Nothing was going to change that.

Soon after his run-in with the Catholic Church John experienced another life changing event. Jim Spillman was invited to speak at his new church in Clawson, Michigan. Spillman told his audience that he had felt compelled to accept this invitation, canceling vacation plans in order to share a very unique message, meant for this group at this time. He told them of a promise that God had made to Jacob's (Israel's) children almost four thousand years ago; to bless them in the last days.

Hidden in the words of Jacob's blessing and revealed in the boundaries of Israel's ancient tribal lands lay the clues to an incredible treasure. A treasure map, taught Spillman, was drafted into the words of the Bible and set into the tribal boundaries of a people who had not yet entered into their promised land. The treasure, a vast oil reserve, was waiting to be discovered in the "latter years" to fulfill God's purpose and provide for his people, Israel.

The Vision

John listened patiently. At first the idea seemed doubtful, a little too far fetched. But, Jim's logic, knowledge of the Bible and maps of Israel's ancient boundaries made for a convincing argument. According to Spillman, God had deposited oil in Israel for some great last days purpose.

John was hooked. Before he left the church in Clawson that night a seed had been planted in his heart. He was convinced that Spillman's message was true He knew, without doubt that the Bible promised a vast treasure of oil for Israel in the last days and pointed to its location. There was oil in Israel and John had just learned where to find it. This knowledge and his unquestioning faith nurtured the seed that would incubate in John's heart for the next two years.

John reflected recently on what Jim Spillman and that night in Clawson meant to him. Starting and ending with scripture, John eulogized Jim's passing and remembered the effect his message had on his life over the last twenty-five years.

> "Then I heard a voice from heaven say, 'Write: Blessed are the dead who die in the Lord from now on.' 'Yes,' says the Spirit, 'they will rest from their labor, for their deeds follow with them'" (Revelation 14:13).

> One of Jim's deeds will be that the revelation that God gave him about the oil of Israel in the '70's will shortly come to pass. Why? Because God sent Jim to Zion temple in Clawson, Michigan in February 1981. Jim taught us the scriptures that proved that oil would someday be found in Israel and on the head of Joseph!

> It was during Jim's teaching that God first deposited the vision in my heart about the oil in Israel and by faith; I believed it (Hebrews 11:1). "Consequently, faith comes from hearing the message, and the message is heard through the words of Christ" (Romans. 10:17). Jim Spillman obeyed God and delivered the message to me in 1981. That vision and God's promises are now coming to pass in Israel.

> "For the revelation awaits an appointed time; it speaks of the end and will not prove false. Though it linger, wait for it; it will certainly come and not delay" (Habakkuk 2:3).

Praying for Oil

John made his first trip to Israel in May of 1983. His friend and mentor, Alger Wolfe accompanied him with the intention of introducing him to an old friend from Texas, Andy SoRelle. SoRelle was an oilman and had been drilling in Israel, near Haifa for the last two years. Like Brown, SoRelle had also heard Jim Spillman's *Treasure* message and set the location of his well site to be in the area known as the "foot of Asher."

During this first trip to Israel John felt God directing him to a specific portion of scripture. Finding his Bible, he paged through the Old Testament until he found the book of I Kings. The passage describing the dedication of the first temple in Jerusalem came from Solomon's prayer:

> Moreover concerning a stranger, that is not of thy people Israel, but cometh out of a far country for thy name's sake: (for they shall hear of thy great name, and of thy strong hand, and of thy stretched out arm); when he shall come and pray towards this house; hear thou in heaven thy dwelling place, and do according to all that the stranger calleth to thee for: that all the people of the earth might know thy name, to fear thee, as do thy people Israel and that they might know that this house, which I have builded, is called by thy name.
>
> (8:41-43)

John saw himself as the "stranger from far country." He believed that if he prayed toward God's temple in Jerusalem, as the passage stated, God would hear him and act according to his prayer, so that, "all the people of the earth would know God and honor His temple."

He asked God for the oil promised to Israel nearly four thousand years earlier. John wanted the oil, not for himself, but for the people and land of Israel. Armed with the scripture

God had given him, he knew by faith that he would be the one to discover Israel's oil.

John stood on the promise he was given. The fact that he was a Michigan tool maker and knew nothing about oil exploration and little about Israel didn't seem to present any obstacle for him. The facts that he had no contacts in the oil business or in Israel didn't bother him a bit. When asked if he felt that his lack of qualifications would slow him down, he simply quoted more scripture; "… by faith I believed I received it … and since then I have by faith spoken it and do not doubt it" (Mark 11:22–24).

Letter of Resignation

Returning to Michigan from his visit to Israel, John drafted, in faith, an open letter of resignation to the people of the company he helped build. Just when they thought they were getting accustomed to the *new* John, his business associates were thrown for another loop by their resident *believer*. The letter left little doubt about where John stood personally and spiritually, and what he intended to do with the rest of his life.

June 1983

TO ALL MY FRIENDS AT GTE VALERON

Now it is with deep regret that I must resign from GTE Valeron. However, I am involved in an oil project that God blessed me with in Israel, and now will devote all of my time in the oil business and doing God's work. Most of you are familiar or know of my past when I was hospitalized four (4) times for alcoholism, but this was all changed dramatically in January 1981 when I was "Saved" or "Born Again." These two (2) terms are not from any denomination, but it is from the Bible and can be found in the New Testament in the book of St. John, Chapter 3 verses 3 through 7. What these terms mean is that I accepted JESUS CHRIST as my Personal Savior. I can testify that I have sat in churches all my life, but I was not "Saved" or "Born Again."

There is no church membership or denomination or water baptism whereby you are 'Born Again" or "Saved," and there is Salvation in no other way but for each person to individually accept JESUS CHRIST as their own personal Savior and Lord of their life. Like St Paul in the New Testament, I was instantly converted and I believe it was to be a witness for you especially here at GTE Valeron, Please don't misunderstand me, as I am not anything special nor did I earn the Salvation, because it cannot be earned as it is a universal gift of God and available to everyone who wants it.

I now pray that each and every one of you will believe that what happened to me is very real and seek the truth for yourselves. Please don't ignore what God is saying to you through me because it is a clear, choice whether you choose JESUS CHRIST as your Personal Savior and receive eternal Salvation, or deny Him and Choose eternal damnation.

I love you all and that is why I'm sending you this,

IN HIS LOVE,

John Brown

John may have worked the longest notice in history. He wrote his resignation in faith; two years later he left Valeron to pursue his vision. Discovering oil in Israel became his full-time quest in December of 1985.

In the years before leaving Valeron, John met Joan Gray. At their first meeting God told John she would be his bride. By faith, he accepted this as fact and told Joan the news. Fortunately, God gave Joan and their pastors similar information.

Joan adopted John's vision in her own way. From their wedding day and every day since Joan sets aside time to pray for the state of Israel and its people.

Houston

John and Joan moved to Houston, Texas in 1986. The move, according to John, was under specific orders from God. He likened the experience to Abraham being called by God away from his homeland to a place "God would show him." John still admits that he doesn't know all the reasons for going to Houston but a procession of events that he could contribute only to the hand of God, confirmed that it was the right move.

Houston was an oil town; and it seemed like a reasonable place to be if one was in the oil business ... even if one's oil business was to be in was in Israel. Now that they had moved to Houston, John began his commute to Israel.

As it turned out, 1986 was not the best time to be in the oil business in Israel. At the beginning of the year the Israeli government suspended all drilling operations in the country for two years in order to conduct a basin analysis study. Anyone in the oil drilling business in Israel was out of business until further notice.

The basin analysis study was essentially a mapping out of the land in terms of geologic basins in order to determine possible locations of oil bearing strata. The study also detailed the history of oil exploration in the country so that future exploration efforts could build on those of the past.

Shutting down oil exploration in Israel for John's first two years in the oil exploration business was the best thing that could have happened to him. Making several trips to Israel during the period, John met with government officials and hired industry consultants in Israel and Texas to conduct research in the areas he knew the oil would be located; the land the Bible describes as "the crown of the head of Joseph."

During the study's down-time John garnered a first rate education in the oil business and created a series of crucial relationships that would later establish him in Israel's oil exploration industry.

Crucial Contact

John met Elisha Roih in 1990. Elisha's personal history paralleled the history of Israel. Born and raised a Palestinian Jew before the State of Israel came into existence, Elisha was part of a small group of Jewish patriots, instrumental in the country's defense before, during and after her independence in 1948. Today *retired* Colonel Elisha Roih is still an active member of the Israeli Defense Forces.

After forty years of experience as a manager in every government owned oil company in Israel, Elisha showed up at John's door in Houston after receiving a letter asking for help. It was as if Israel had sent John a guardian angel.

Amazed that one of Israel's oil pioneers would materialize on his doorstep in Houston, John asked incredulously; "What are you doing here?"

Elisha smiled and shrugged in his uniquely Israeli way. "I've come to help," he replied. And that was it. He *adopted* John and his vision. With Elisha's help, John was introduced and accepted into Israel's oil industry. Today, Elisha Roih serves as Vice President, Administration of Israeli Operations for Zion Oil & Gas, Inc.

Raising Capital

Spending his own money searching for Israel's oil was a non-issue for John. From the day he received the vision through his last days living in Houston, John invested every dollar and every moment of his time in the search.

Other investors, however, were few and far between. John wasn't alone in underwriting his oil exploration efforts in Israel but the group of friends willing to contribute money, time and prayers was small. One friend, Ralph DeVore, helped and encouraged John from the beginning. Among Ralph's contributions was introducing John to his cousin, Bible prophecy teacher Hal Lindsay. Hal included John's story in his weekly television program, commenting that the discovery of oil in Israel could be the prophetic fulfillment of Ezekiel 38. Hal Lindsay remains an avid supporter of Zion Oil today.

John was baffled by the response he received from audiences worldwide when trying to raise money for his venture. To him the proposition was perfectly straight-forward. According to scripture, God put a vast oil deposit deep under the land of Israel. God's intention was that this oil be discovered and brought to the surface as a latter day blessing to the people of Israel. Surely, he thought, any friend of Israel would understand the importance of this mission and enthusiastically invest in making it a reality!

The Jewish Community

John took the story of his mission to America's Jewish community. A major oil discovery in Israel would assure her energy independence and prosperity. He was positive that the Jewish community in America would be the first to support his efforts in Israel.

To his disappointment, the Jewish community didn't get on board. Most American Jews favor a strong and prosperous Israel. They are the first and most generous donors to Israel. However, investing in the oil company of a gentile Christian Zionist wasn't necessarily considered "mitzvah."

Mitzvah means literally "commandment"; and in the Jewish community has come to mean a *good deed* or a *blessing.* If Jewish Americans want to help Jews in Israel, they give to Jewish Israeli causes; that's mitzvah. Raising money for some gentile whose goal is to discover oil in Israel? Well ...?

The Christian Community

If the Jewish community couldn't understand the importance of his vision, he believed that surely the Christian community would. What Christian wouldn't want to see Israel blessed by a mammoth oil discovery?

John spoke to evangelical Christian groups and the response was mixed. A lot of Christians listened, believed the message and backed the effort. Others figured it was just another scam in the name of helping Israel.

Unfortunately, John wasn't the first to ask American Christians to invest money in finding Israel's oil. In the years John had been spending his own money in the search, other "Christian" oil men were preaching the same message of investing in the search for Israel's oil. Some of these evangelical oil pitchmen were sincere and some were flat out crooks. Either way, investors lost their money.

The honest oil men drilled, hoping to find the oil promised to Jacob's heirs, but came up broke, with nothing to show but a few dry holes. The crooks took the money and ran. Investing in the search for Israel's oil was starting to leave a bad taste in the mouths of America's Christians. Whether they invested with the honest ones or the crooked, everybody lost money.

Evangelicals were growing weary of seeing their money go down dry holes. They expected results. No oil flowed from the land of Israel and the vision of Jacob's blessing was beginning to fade. John's mission became just another cause on a long list of Christian causes.

Hitting the Bottom

A decade of full time vision quest for John Brown resulted in being broke, really broke. He had traveled to Israel numerous times in the last ten years. He spent every dime he had, working to make his vision a reality. He had traveled across America, telling his story and spreading his vision. Now, in 1996, ten years after committing himself full-time to *God's work*, he was broke, destitute, and stuck in Houston.

John was done with the oil business, done with Israel, done with throwing his money, time and energy into a vision that always seemed to be just beyond his reach. He was ready to admit defeat, go home to Michigan, and pick up what was left of his life. Unfortunately, he was too broke to even give up and go home.

The next several months in Houston gave John an opportunity to reflect on his *Vision* and his whirlwind ride over the last ten years. It also gave him a chance to experience life at the end of his own strength and capital. He worked part time as a custodian, cleaning bathrooms in his church. He and Joan didn't even have money for groceries; they certainly couldn't afford to search for oil. If oil was to be discovered in Israel, it was going to have to be someone else doing the discovering. John was done.

Restored

Back in Michigan, John's son, Mark was involved in a small concrete forming business. John didn't know anything about concrete forming and he didn't have the money to return to Michigan. But the facts had a way of getting swept downstream whenever God was ready to do something in John's life. The cash for a one-way trip to Michigan was miraculously put into their hands and he and Joan moved back to Michigan.

Like everything he'd ever done, John jumped into the concrete business with both feet. Within eighteen months the M&B companies had produced over $8 million in new sales, nearly $1 million in profits, and a $1.5 million credit line.

During John's time in Michigan, God made it clear to him that He had no intention of reneging on His promise. God wasn't allowing him a *semi-retirement* into the concrete business. It was time to renew his search for oil in Israel.

CHAPTER THIRTEEN

ZION OIL

The ballroom of the Hotel Palomar in Dallas was filled to capacity. People had come from around North America, from Israel, from Europe and further abroad. Those in attendance were as varied as their points of origin. International businessmen, homegrown entrepreneurs, rabbis, ministers, retirees and housewives all assembled to witness the beginnings of something that had become a part of their lives.

These were the friends and investors of Zion Oil. Some had only recently become a part of the Zion story; others had been with John Brown when all he owned was a Bible and the faith that God would one day fulfill His promise to Jacob's children.

Investors with hundreds of thousands of dollars at stake sat together with retired couples who had put in everything they could, the minimum seven hundred dollars. As varied as this assembly was, they shared one thing - John Brown's vision, that they would see oil flowing in the land of Israel.

It was June 19, 2007. Zion Oil & Gas, Inc. was holding its first stockholders meeting as a publicly traded company. They had raised more than $12.6 million in a successful initial public offering and Zion Oil & Gas was now trading on the American Stock Exchange under the symbol ZN.

The mood in the room was like that of a graduation ceremony. Formality governed the proceedings and a sense that something momentous was happening hung in the air. Zion was moving to another level.

A New Chapter

With Zion's successful IPO the scenery of the story had changed. In the history of Israel's Bible based oil hunters, the central figure was always a lone visionary, taking his faith in God's Word as guarantee, throwing his life and fortune into finding a treasure promised to the children of Israel nearly four thousand years ago.

Always haunted by limited financial, physical and professional resources, there was only so much the individual explorers could accomplish. Often, they had the help and support of friends, but this was essentially a solitary mission. The burden of faith and grit always came home to the shoulders of the man with the vision.

Now, for the first time the weight of the work at hand sat on corporate shoulders. John Brown remained the visionary, the company's compass, but now his vision had caught fire and Zion's mission was borne by a team of talented professionals and hundreds of investors; all sharing the vision of bringing the prophecy of Israel's oil into reality. Zion Oil had entered into another stage of its life.

John Brown addressed the assembly of investors and management, telling them the story of Elijah praying for rain.[1] Before he prayed, Elijah told the king to get up and go home because, "... there is a sound of abundance of rain."

---

[1] I Kings 18: 41-46

Elijah sent his servant to look for clouds six times and six times there was no sign of rain. He sent him out a seventh time and the tiniest of clouds appeared on the horizon, growing as it came until it brought a great storm. Elijah knew his request had been answered before he prayed it; he was just waiting for the physical evidence to catch up.

John finished his story and looked out over the audience. He saw old friends who had supported him from the beginning, new friends who had adopted the vision of Israel's oil as their own and investors who regarded their stake as something more than just another business venture. He sent them home with a final word. "What I see here is the prophecy fulfilled. I hear the sound of abundance and it's not rain; it's oil and lots of it."

Beginnings

It had been a long road since the day seven years earlier when Zion Oil & Gas Company had first received its incorporation papers. In the beginning Zion's ownership consisted of twenty-five friends and partners; all having supported John's lone vision quest over the years. The start up capital of $2400 became 2,400,000 shares of stock, valued at one-tenth of one cent per share.

Everything John and his partners had contributed over the previous fifteen years was thrown into the pot. There was no way to calculate the dollar value of the technical, legal and financial contribution accumulated over the years but it was easily in the millions.

A tremendous amount of work and progress had transpired in the years between Zion's start up and this day in Dallas seven years later. Zion had moved to another level, but the reason for the company's existence remained constant; embodied in Zion's Purpose Statement:

Zion Oil & Gas was ordained by G_d for the express purpose of discovering oil and gas in the land of Israel and to bless the Jewish people and the nation of Israel and the body of Christ (Isaiah 23:18). I believe that G_d has promised in the Bible to bless Israel with one of the world's largest oil and gas fields and this will be discovered in the last days before the Messiah returns and that it will be found on the Ma'anit License and the Joseph permit, both being on the head of Joseph. [2]

Team Zion

What began as one man's vision quest has grown into a corporate purpose. The talent and experience of Zion's management team, even skeptics admit, is remarkable. With more than 200 years of combined oil industry experience, Zion's management represents a dream team that any of the world's major oil companies would love to get their hands on.

Two aspects of the Zion team stand out; they seem to have been hand picked from the world's top talent in their respective fields of expertise and they share a personal mission to see the Zion Oil vision fulfilled.

Some of the team members were ready to join before the organization itself came into being. A few have moved on, having fulfilled their unique purpose in the Zion Oil story. Others have joined Zion recently; their talents fitting hand in glove with the organization's needs. This phenomenon has been a part of the company's history; each team member comes to Zion with a unique expertise and experience in order to fulfill a specific purpose with what continues to appear perfect timing. John Brown says God put the team together. After reading their résumés and hearing their stories most folks think John may just be right.

---

[2] See Appendix A for Zion's Vision and Purpose Statement.

Richard Rinberg

Zion's CEO makes an immediate impression. The epitome of a modern English gentleman; his resume includes membership in the London Diamond Bourse and the legendary Lloyd's of London. Rinberg handles problems, praise and the press with a balance of elegance and common sense, winning the confidence of those around him as he goes.

According to Richard, he waded into the company, "bit by bit." Richard began quietly investing in Zion Oil in 2004, he explains in his understated way; "… a bit, then a bit more, then a bit more."

Due to his financial involvement and his gift of solving business problems brilliantly and calmly, Zion asked for his counsel on an issue they were experiencing in Israel. Richard gave his advice, Zion's problem found a solution and Richard found himself acting as the company's de-facto arbiter. Soon afterward, John Brown, following what he believed was God's lead, asked Richard to become Zion's president.

Richard wasn't looking for a job. Having made *aliyah* (immigrated) to Israel from London, Richard had planned a peaceful semi-retirement; quietly investing in worthy projects. He had no idea that one of his worthy projects would require more than just his money.

Before his move to Israel Richard had survived a virulent strep pneumonia, requiring surgery and months of recuperation. After this potentially fatal health scare he made the commitment, both maritally and spiritually that he would never again allow business concerns to control his personal welfare. It was a commitment his wife, Emma, meant for him to keep.

John Brown knew in his heart that God had led Richard into the company but he was sensitive to the

Rinbergs' needs and committed that as President, Richard would not be required to work more than two hours a day.

Richard, true to form, performed brilliantly and calmly, and true to his previous experience with Zion Oil, found himself wading in "a bit" further. Richard Rinberg became CEO of Zion Oil & Gas Company in March of 2007, replacing the retiring CEO Gene Soltero.

Today Richard and Zion still hold to the original commitment of two-hours per day. Most days, however, two hours last much longer than others …with Emma's approval.

Philip Mandelker

John Brown and Israeli attorney Philip Mandelker met in 1998. Philip's background in petroleum law, both in the U.S. and Israel is extensive and he is regarded by his peers as one of Israel's premier oil and gas experts. Mandelker was instrumental in John Brown becoming established in Israel's oil industry. With Philip's help, John formed Zion Oil & Gas, Inc. in April of 2000 and was awarded a small (28,800 acre) onshore petroleum license from the Israeli government.

When Zion became a company, Philip became the company's General Counsel; leading it through the legal jungle of private investment and later, through the flood of Securities and Exchange Commission requirements that led to Zion's successful initial public offering in 2007. Today Philip serves as Zion's Executive Vice-President.

Notwithstanding his legal and professional involvement in the company, Philip made another unique contribution to the Zion Oil story. In 2005 Mandelker published a paper presenting biblical and historical references to petroleum oil in ancient Israel and successfully argued that scriptures containing prophetic references to the "blessings of the deep" may indeed refer to a petroleum reserve.

Beyond its scholarship and historical proof that olive oil wasn't the only *oil* known in the ancient lands of the Bible, it presented the related scriptures and history from a uniquely Jewish perspective. The paper is a powerful reminder to Christians that the Bible is a Jewish document and that our understanding of ancient Israel benefits greatly by looking through the lens of a scholar of modern Israel.

"The Search for Oil in the Land of Israel – A Biblical Treasure Hunt" by Philip Mandelker is available in electronic format at (www.zionoil.com) or at www.OilinIsrael.net.

Glen Perry

Zion's President, Glen Perry is a sinewy soft spoken Tennessean. His ruddy complexion is more reminiscent of a cowboy than a corporate executive. Nobody in the boardroom seems to mind though; he also happens to be one of the world's leading petroleum professionals.

Glen's early experience included stints with the world's largest oil companies, including Exxon (now ExxonMobil) and Energy Reserves Group (now BHP). After Exxon and ERG, Glen earned industry recognition as a world class oil man during his career at Prairie Producing Company, now a part of UNOCAL.

After his corporate retirement in 1990, Glen took a role in developing oilfields in the former Soviet Republic and consulted on the exploration that produced Israel's huge off-shore natural gas discovery. It is the production from this gas reserve that now fuels many of Israel's electrical generation plants. Glen also advised on the recent 2006 Dead Sea oil discovery; a reserve estimated at four to six million barrels.

At their first meeting in 1999, Glen was fascinated by John Brown's vision for oil in Israel but he needed geological evidence to back up John's biblical clues. John commissioned Glen, and later, Israeli geologist Dr. Eliezer Kashai to perform preliminary research "below the foot of Asher" and on the "crown of the head of Joseph"; the area in and around the current day Kibbutz Ma'anit.

Glen Perry found his geological evidence in the Ma'anit structure, on the biblical "head of Joseph" - right where Jacob and Moses, almost four thousand years ago, prophesied it to be.

Glen has been a part Zion Oil & Gas full time since April of 2000, currently serving both as director and president; running the company's Israeli operations.

In an interview with the Israeli newspaper Haaretz about Zion's vision for oil in Israel Glen commented:

> People who say there is no oil in Israel speak out of ignorance. It's the biblical aspect that brought John (Brown), but our team has looked purely at the technical aspects of this project.

Eliezer Kashai

If the history of Israeli oil exploration could be boiled down to a single person, it would be Dr. Eliezer Kashai. Dr Kashai has been present for the beginning, middle, and end of every significant Israeli led oil exploration effort in the country since 1959.

From 1959 to 1975 he served in progressively increasing roles, from senior geologist to chief geologist at Lapidoth, the Israeli government owned oil drilling entity. Oil Exploration Investment, Ltd., Israel's government owned oil exploration company employed Dr. Kashai first as chief geologist, then as managing director. During his tenure as managing director of OEIL, Dr. Kashai was the official responsible for Israel's search for oil. After his *retirement* in 1987, Dr. Kashai served as an exploration consultant for the major private and government oil exploration efforts in the country, including the original geologic interpretation of

Ma'anit 1, the well reopened by Zion Oil as part of the Joseph project.

In his fifty years as an oil geologist, Dr. Kashai has served as president of the Israeli Geological Society, and has published most of the geologic data relating to the country's potential oil reserves. Since October 2000 Dr. Kashai has served as Zion Oil's Vice-President of Israeli Exploration.

Stephen Pierce

In 1980 the State of Israel commissioned Stephen Pierce (as an employee of Superior Oil Company) to conduct and publish a Basin Analysis Study of the country. In an exhaustive eighteen month study involving hundreds of kilometers of seismic tests, reprocessing hundreds of additional kilometers of existing test data, and analysis of data from the country's existing deep well Stephen was able to publish some very specific conclusions. The top three oil reserve prospects in the country were:

1. Off-shore, just off the coast of Haifa, the land known as the *"foot of Asher"*

2. The kibbutz Ma'anit area.

3. A site in Zion's current license area known as the Joseph 1 prospect area.

The study was a seminal work in Israel's oil history, being the first single document to consolidate all existing information and comprehensively identify Israel's greatest oil prospect areas.

In May of 2004 Stephen was commissioned to publish an additional independent study targeting the Ma'anit and Joseph license area. Confirming that geological evidence for oil reserves in the region is overwhelming; and noting that oil has recently been discovered just south of the license he praises Zion's prudent approach:

Zion has correctly adduced that there is a high probability of discovering a small commercial discovery and a correspondingly low probability of finding a large discovery. These conservative values are a welcome change from those provided by promoters that offer great rewards and severely underplay the risks.

His conclusion to the study regarding Zion's license area is equally positive:

It is our opinion that Zion has reasonably evaluated the hydrocarbon potential of the Ma'anit – Joseph License and that they have analyzed and presented two drillable oil and gas exploration prospects consistent with the highest professional standards of the international oil industry. Given the risks that always accompany drilling oil wells, Zion has undertaken a better than normal due diligence in presenting the petroleum exploration prospects of the Ma'anit – Joseph License, Israel.

Credited with perhaps the most significant industry appraisal of Israel's oil prospects in the last fifty years, Stephen's article in the July 5, 2004 in the *"Oil & Gas Journal"* ran concurrently with news of Israel's first substantial onshore oil find, Givot Olam's Meged 4 well, just south of Zion's license area.

Stephen Pierce, the geologist that virtually mapped Israel's oil prospects, petitioned Zion Oil in 2005 to consider taking him on as a team member. He now serves as Zion Oil's Exploration Manager.

*****

Each Zion team member has been *called* into the company. CFO Martin Van Brauman, Executive Vice President William Avery, Vice President and Chief Accounting Officer Sandra Green, Marketing Manager Don Weitz and Geologist Aaron Kahn all have their own stories of how they believe God drew them into Zion. They can only believe they are part of a special destiny. Like Esther in days of old, "And who knows whether you have not come to the kingdom for such a time as this?"(Esther 4: 14b ESV)

The Joseph Project

Zion received its first oil and gas exploration license in May of 2000. The Ma'anit License consisted of 28,800 acres in northern Israel, geologic data from previous petroleum exploration in the permit area and an abandoned well, the Ma'anit 1.

By January of 2003 Zion had extended its license area, renamed the Ma'anit-Joseph License, to encompass 95,800 acres, including the original 28,800 acre Ma'anit License.

In August of 2005 Zion was also awarded the Asher preliminary exploration permit. The Asher permit area included 121,000 acres surrounding the Carmel/Haifa region, the *foot of Asher*. By January 2007 this preliminary permit was converted to an exploration license, renamed the Asher-Menashe License, containing 84,000 acres.

Zion's Joseph License, formerly the Ma'anit-Joseph License, currently in a release and reapplication process will include 85,000 acres of the original 95,800 acre license. The Joseph license area, south of the Asher-Menashe License, includes the Ma'anit 1 well site and the Ma'anit Rehoboth well site. Located between Tel Aviv and Haifa, the Joseph License, biblically speaking, lies in the tribal territory of Manasseh on the "crown of the head of Joseph."

The map on the following page depicts an overlay of location of the Asher-Menashe and Joseph License areas. This license area lies just south of the "foot of Asher" and consists of a substantial portion of Manasseh's tribal boundaries, the "crown of the head of Joseph."

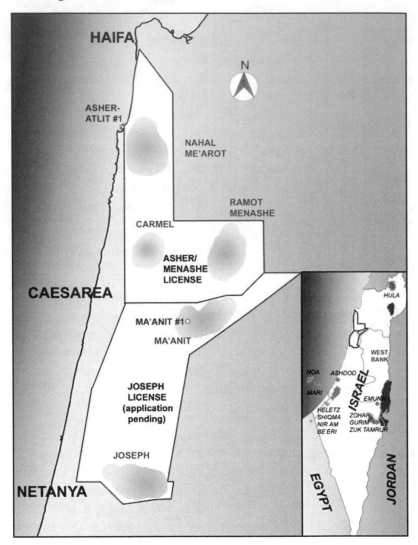

Ma'anit 1

Zion's first oil drilling project was to reopen and deepen an existing well near the Kibbutz Ma'anit. The well, Ma'anit 1, was originally drilled to a depth of 7,651 feet in 1995 (with no substantial shows of oil or gas) before shutting down for lack of funds.

According to geologists, the well, one of only a few in the region, just wasn't deep enough. Of the 420 wells drilled in Israel, only eight were located in the north, and only five of those could be considered truly exploratory. According to Zion Oil President Glen Perry, there is … "only one deep well per 1500 square kilometers in Northern Israel and that makes the area vastly under explored."

The 7,651 foot depth of the original Ma'anit 1 only reached to the late Jurassic era rock. Rock strata from this period aren't geologically favorable for storing hydrocarbons. The geology of the late Jurassic era in this part of Israel consists of dolomitic limestone; all in all it is pretty close packed stuff. There isn't much room for oil.

Reservoir Rock

In order to store oil in rock, there must be some free space in the strata where it's to be stored; what oil geologists call *reservoir rock*. Tightly packed dolomitic limestone doesn't contain empty spaces sufficient for storing oil, so no appreciable oil can collect there.

Below the Jurassic period rock, however, the geologic conditions are more favorable for storing oil. Unlike limestone, Triassic era dolomite doesn't crush under pressure, retaining much of its original porosity and permeability. Its structure is like a network of tiny pipes connecting the holes in the rock. This complex of natural connecting "pipes" and holes allows Triassic dolomite to both hold (porosity) and transport (permeability) oil. Triassic dolomite can hold up to twenty times more oil and gas deposits as the Jurassic era limestone above it.

The problem with the original Ma'anit 1, like most of the wells before it, was that it never reached oil bearing rock – it just wasn't deep enough.

Triassic Oil

Zion calculated that if they entered the original Ma'anit 1 well and drilled an additional 5,472 feet, they would reach geology from the late Triassic era. Geologists believe that the Ma'anit region was once a part of the shoreline of an ancient sea. This shallow, high energy shoreline produced coral reef structures. These ancient coral reefs, through the ages, become porous dolomites, ideal for the development of potential oil reserves. According to seismic studies, the thickness of the porous structure below the Ma'anit well has been estimated at thirteen hundred feet.

When I learned that geologists estimated the porous structure at thirteen hundred feet thick I assumed that this was a good thing but I didn't really know. I consulted with then Zion President and CEO Gene Soltero. He used the term "vertical column" to describe, in oil drilling terms, how much harvestable depth (thickness of oil-bearing rock) a potential profitable site contained. I asked him if thirteen hundred feet of *vertical column* was a lot.

Gene smiled as if he'd just been asked, "Is Christmas a big holiday for kids?"

"Here in Texas," Gene replied, "we consider a well with thirty feet of vertical column to be a success." From that statement I gathered that thirteen hundred feet of vertical column is a lot of hole from which to pump oil.

Source Rock

In addition to reservoir rock, an oil prospect also needs, somewhere in its history, something from which to make oil. Oil, comes from ancient plants and animals. These plants and animals die and eventually get buried by sediment; the sediment compresses and gets hot eventually becoming sedimentary rock, what oil geologists call *source rock*.

All living things, plants and animals, are made up of carbon compounds. When they die, the carbon compounds break down and link to hydrogen atoms to form hydrocarbons. Oil and gas reserves (hydrocarbons) are the result of the carbon contained in ancient plants and animals going through this natural chemical process.

According to Frank Stoakes, a world expert on reefs, the Triassic era lagoon that produced the reef structure below Ma'anit also produced a tremendous amount of algae; this plant matter, when it died and sank to the bottom, produced carbon as it was compressed into the sediment, eventually becoming crude oil and natural gas.

The Triassic era algae are just one of several sources of potential hydrocarbons lying beneath Ma'anit. As Zion's engineers were to discover later, hydrocarbons from a deeper source, formed much earlier than the Triassic era oil, existed in the rock beneath Ma'anit 1.

The Seal

The final thing an oil prospect needs is a seal; a lid that keeps the oil in one place until man can discover it, drill a well and bring it to the surface. Since oil and gas is lighter than water (in most cases) and since reservoir rock is usually filled with water, the oil and gas will rise, floating up over time through natural fractures in the subsurface rocks, eventually displacing the water in the reservoir rocks.

The seal, or a cap, above the reservoir rock keeps the oil and gas from migrating any further, so it will collect in the reservoir rock in sufficient quantities to make getting at it worth while. Remember all that tightly packed dolomitic limestone up in the Jurassic era? The Jurassic limestone structure that prevented any worthwhile oil and gas discoveries turned out to be the perfect seal for holding the deeper oil and gas reservoirs in place!

Drilling Begins

Only one rig in Israel exists capable of drilling deep enough to reach the Triassic oil reserves. The Ideco Super 7-11, owned by Israel's Lapidoth Drilling Company is the largest drilling rig in the country. On April 3, 2005 the Ideco rig stood center stage as Rabbi Yitsak Swartz pronounced his blessing at the public dedication of the reopening of Ma'anit 1, citing a Deuteronomy 33:19:

> They shall call the people unto the mountain; there they shall offer sacrifices of righteousness; for they shall suck of the abundance of the seas, and of treasures hid in the sand".

During the summer of 2005, using the Lapidoth rig, Zion Oil & Gas deepened the hole at Ma'anit 1 according to plan, penetrating the Triassic era formations. What they found there was far more important in the long run than what they didn't find.

Permian!

Oil and gas deposits showed up in the Triassic, just as they had expected. What they didn't expect was that Triassic age sediments started showing up at 10,833 feet; nearly 2,000 feet closer to the surface than their data had indicated. This meant that Permian strata from the Paleozoic era, the layer beneath the Triassic and the world's most prolific oil bearing strata, was 2,000 feet closer than they had thought!

Zion had always focused their exploration efforts on the Triassic era oil reserves because, according to existing geological data, that the far more productive Permian reserves were out of reach.

This was fantastic news; Zion could adjust their plan, deepen the well and go for Permian oil! Instead of stopping at

13,123 feet as originally planned, they continued drilling through Triassic rock, on their way to the Permian.

Problems in the Hole

At 15,842 feet, only 330 feet above the projected depth of Permian rock, they stopped drilling. They had encountered problems in the hole. Difficult rock strata and drill pipe failures meant that going any further would risk a *twist off*.

A *twist off* meant loosing the hole due to the drill head getting stuck and twisting off the main shaft, possibly taking hundreds of feet of drill pipe with it. Having a drill head and length off shaft forever stuck in bottom of the hole rendered the well useless for further drilling or production below the twist off point.

It was safer to stop drilling and develop the hole they had rather than risk a twist off. Zion's team stopped drilling at 15,842 feet and began to plan their next move.

Signs from Above

Some controversy among Zion's managers was brewing over what to do with the hole. Should they proceed with Ma'anit 1, developing the hole they had for production or should they move to a new sight close by, one that had been mapped as an even better prospect than Ma'anit 1?

John Brown seeks his direction from God and God gives him direction, through scripture. This time was no different. John's answer came from Genesis 26:22:

> And he moved from there and dug another well, and they did not quarrel over it. So he called its name Rehoboth, because he said, "For now the LORD has made room for us, and we shall be fruitful in the land."

John knew that whatever they decided about Ma'anit 1, there would be another well. As if to bring the point home,

God sent John another message and the messenger certainly wasn't what John was expecting.

The Bratzlav Hasidim

John was staying at the kibbutz Ma'anit, adjacent to the well site while they were figuring out what to do with Ma'anit 1. Late one night he awoke to someone knocking on the door to his room. John opened the door to find two men dressed in black coats, wearing black fedoras on their heads, with long side locks of hair spilling from under their hats. These were Hasidim, ultra-orthodox Jews.

The men requested that John accompany them to Jerusalem for an audience with the Rabbi Eliezer Berland. John didn't know who these men were and had never heard of Rabbi Berland. He refused to go anywhere with two strange men at this time of night, but he said that he would check out their story and get back in touch with them.

Rabbi Berland, John discovered, was the Dean of Shuvu Banim Yeshiva in Jerusalem and a leading Rabbi of the Bratzlav Hasidic court, an ultra-orthodox Jewish sect with thousands of followers throughout the world. John agreed to meet the Rabbi at the Yeshiva in Jerusalem.

Rabbi Berland, it turns out, had been monitoring Zion's activities at Ma'anit and had become a fan. He told John that he believed Zion would meet with success, but, according to scripture, the oil was deep beneath the surface and his efforts should be directed deeper.

Rabbi Berland invited John to return to the Yeshiva at which time he would pronounce a "Bracha," or blessing over Zion. The Bracha of an esteemed Rabbi is no light matter in orthodox Judaism. It is meant to be taken literally and seriously. Rabbi Berland's blessing, according to the Bratzlav Hasidim assured Zion of G_d's favor in their mission:

With Heaven's Help

To the Honored Zion Oil & Gas, Inc.
Greetings, a Blessing and All Good Things, Sela

By these presents we bless your company that you shall
find an abundance of oil and gas and that there shall be
naturally flowing fountains of oil that will suffice for the
whole world. And by grace of this, we will be able to
build the Temple in the twinkling of an eye.

Amen [so be it] for eternity, Sela

An ultra-orthodox Rabbi enthusiastically supporting a
gentile Christian oil man from Dallas? A strange affection ...
unless you stop to consider that they may be getting their
instructions from a common Source.

Developing Ma'anit 1

Zion made the decision to develop Ma'anit 1 before
moving on to the next drill site. There were promising oil and
gas shows deeper in the hole and they believe they could coax
some production out of this well.

Zion's engineers tested the lowest section of the well.
At 15,223 feet they brought up nothing but heavy salt water.
At 15,128 feet they also found water, this time with oil
floating on top. It was time for a judgment call.

Due to the proximity and amount of water and the
relatively thin layer of oil, they chose to abandon the lowest
zone and test higher in the hole. Testing again at 14,245 to
14,593 feet, the hydrocarbon results were positive; but again
they ran into salt water. Zion's managers knew that extracting
the salt water to get at the hydrocarbons would be time
consuming and expensive. They made the decision to go
higher.

Still in the Triassic they made a third attempt. Drilling
data had shown a potentially productive region between

12,559 feet and 13,125 feet that could possibly hold 250 feet of hydrocarbon bearing rock. They plugged the well below 13,125 feet and perforated the casing just above to find out what it held. Water again!

After several weeks of cementing operations Zion's engineers determined that what they thought was possible hydrocarbon bearing rock in the zone contained only water.

Knowing that the possibility of encountering significant oil and gas deposits shrank as they worked their way up the hole, they made a final play. Go back down the hole to just under 14,000 feet, attempt to shut off the water and harvest the existing hydrocarbons.

This time they were able to seal off the water in the region and back flush the hole to see what they had. During the back flush operation they maintained a six to ten foot gas flair at the well head; this was a very good sign. After the back flush operation they shut down the rig for a month to analyze their results and let hydrocarbons collect in the well. In thirty days they returned to the zone that had produced the gas flares and found that a cement seal had broken and water had once again flooded the hole.

They weren't giving up, but it was time to release the Lapidoth rig. They would analyze their data before scheduling a *workover* rig to prepare the hole for what they hoped would be their first oil production.

Plan B

Zion's team spent 2006 analyzing data from Ma'anit 1 and raising capital for future drilling operations. No drilling took place that year but Zion's Israel offices were operating at full tilt analyzing data and Dallas was working overtime preparing for their upcoming IPO.

Zion Oil & Gas literally rang in the New Year, as the first company of 2007 to ring the bell at the American Stock Exchange; going public under the ZN ticker symbol.

By April of 2007 Lapidoth's workover equipment had arrived at the Ma'anit 1 well site. The plan was to re-enter the well to begin workover operations in the four upper zones that they believed to hold oil and gas and were sufficiently above the troublesome water bearing zones they had encountered earlier. For two months, the Zion field team worked the well and analyzed the results. In the end, on the eve of Zion's first stockholder's meeting as a public company, Zion made their findings public.

> [The] geological and engineering team have completed its analysis of the test results of the first four zones in the upper Triassic which had been identified as potentially productive and selected for testing during the immediate workover and completion operations on the company's Ma'anit #1 well. The results of the test indicated that the tested zone is non-productive.

Non-productive. The announcement sat like a stone on the hearts of those who had waited expectantly for the prophecy of Israel's oil to be fulfilled. Was the Ma'anit 1 just another dry hole? Was John Brown just the last in a string of failed Bible based oil hunters in the Holy Land?

Not according to John Brown, who, by faith, sees the prophecy as already fulfilled. He knows the oil is there, where God put it, waiting for the appropriate time.

Not according to Zion's engineering team. They had seen oil and gas in the middle and lower Triassic during the drilling and testing operations. More importantly, they had brought up traces of oil from the deeper Permian section of the Paleozoic era.

Permian strata on the northeast side of the Arabian Peninsula contain twenty-five percent of all of the world's known natural gas. So far at least 23 oil and gas fields have been found on the edge of the peninsula and the Zion exploration staff believes that Israel, which sits on the northwest side of the peninsula, may very well have the next.

The prolific section of the Permian is estimated to be about 1500 feet below the bottom of the Ma'anit #1. They know the oil is there because they've seen it, and they intend to bring it to the surface.

Ma'anit 1 is by no means a dead issue. They already own 15,842 feet of open hole; rock they won't need to drill through again. The drilling problems encountered in 2005 must be overcome, perhaps with better equipment or techniques, but it could be done. By going back down into the Ma'anit 1 hole and drilling deeper, Zion could very well have its first productive well.

Another option is to begin drilling on the Ma'anit Rehoboth site only 500 yards from the Ma'anit 1 well. According to seismic data the Rehoboth site sits on a "geologic high." This means that the Permian is higher under Ma'anit Rehoboth than it is under Ma'anit 1. Drilling operations will reach the Permian sooner than what they experienced at Ma'anit 1. Zion's project plan for Ma'anit Rehoboth is to target the Permian; drilling to a depth 18,100 feet.

The investment in Ma'anit 1 shouldn't be considered wasted. The well was considered a "rank wildcat." This means that the seismic data for the area indicated good prospects, but there was really no way of knowing exactly what was down there until they drilled.

The drilling of Ma'anit 1 provided invaluable data and experience for future exploration operations and may yet prove to be a productive oil well if deeper oil reserves can be accessed.

Whether the decision is made to first reenter Ma'anit 1 or to begin drilling the Ma'anit Rehoboth site, the results from the 2005 and 2006 drilling and completion operations will have a profound impact on future operations.

The two key lessons learned from Ma'anit 1 were that: 1) there is oil deep beneath the land of Manasseh, and 2) The Permian is closer and more accessible than anyone had previously imagined.

Equipment

One shortcoming that continues to haunt oil exploration operations in northern Israel is that of equipment.

Zion can use over 11,000 feet of their existing wellbore in Ma'anit 1 and then drill directionally from that depth to a target 2000 to 2500 feet north of the well; an optimum position to test the Permian.

Lapidoth's Ideco Super 7-11 is the largest drilling rig in the country and up to this point, the only one capable of handling Zion's requirements. Even then, the rig is at its mechanical limits at depths necessary to explore deep petroleum prospects.

In order to truly have control over their exploration and drilling operations, Zion must consider purchasing their own drilling equipment.

The decision to stop drilling the Ma'anit 1 at 15,842 feet wasn't that Zion had run out of money or that they believed they were deep enough, they knew they weren't. Drilling ceased at Ma'anit 1 because at that depth, using Lapidoth's equipment, Zion's engineers were afraid they would lose the well.

Zion's team now knows that the oil rich Permian is reachable. They know that the deeper they drill the more oil shows they encounter. Zion's future operations will be at depths beyond the 15,842 feet mark of Ma'anit 1.

Zion's expanded license area and exploration efforts have grown them into a multi-well project plan, now having identified eleven new potential drilling prospects. In order to control their drilling destiny, Zion must control their drilling equipment.

Plans are underway to move Zion to the next level of oil exploration and production capability, either by purchasing drilling equipment or entering into a long term contract with a reliable drilling contractor whose equipment is capable of reaching at least 20,000 feet.

Moving Forward

Because of the shortage of suitable drilling equipment, Zion hopes to resume drilling operations in late 2007 or early 2008. Most of the equipment is being delivered as this book goes to print and Zion says that they will be ready as soon as there is a suitable drilling rig. Most likely, the Ma'anit-Rehoboth #2 will be drilled directionally from the Ma'anit #1 wellbore in an effort to reduce the overall time and cost. By drilling directionally, Zion can penetrate the Permian at what is believed to be the optimum location to hit the Permian reservoirs.

*****

God is keeping His promise to Jacob; his children will *suck oil from the rock.* In his heart and mind John Brown knows that the prophecy has already been fulfilled; it's only a matter of time.

The discovery of oil in the ancient lands of Manasseh and Asher, whenever it comes and whichever well it first flows from, will be the fulfillment of two promises; one to John Brown, a Michigan tool maker, simple enough in his belief to take God at his word and another to Israel's children almost four-thousand years ago, that in the last days they would inherit the "blessings of the deep" and "treasures hid in the sand."

Map No. 3584 Rev. 2   UNITED NATIONS
January 2004

Department of Peacekeeping Operations
Cartographic Section

1

---

[1] Source: UN Cartographic Section Map 3584 Rev 2

CHAPTER FOURTEEN

ISRAEL TODAY

Slightly smaller than the state of New Jersey, most of Israel's land mass is desert. Virtually all economic and agricultural activity takes place in the central and northern parts of the country, between narrow borders; squeezed on the west by the Mediterranean Sea and on the east by the Palestinians, Jordan, and Syria.

With as few natural resource options as she was given, Israel has made the most of them. In between wars and continued harassment by her enemy neighbors she has created an oasis out of desert and an economy from sand, sweat and blood.

The Economy

Israel's economy has taken a beating in recent years. Tourism, High-technology, diamond cutting, and agriculture are the mainstays of Israel's economy. Israel is *The Holy Land* for Christians, Jews, and Moslems around the world. Every year the country has counted on religious pilgrims and their tourist dollars as an economic staple. The threat of increased terrorism in Israel and around the world has all but killed Israeli tourism.

High-technology and diamond cutting continue to be core competencies for Israel's but industry in general has suffered a sharp decline in foreign investment due to concern over increasing terror activities.

Agriculture is a bright spot in Israel's economy. Israel has successfully turned her deserts into gardens; feeding the nation and exporting much of its produce to European markets. Unfortunately, even a thriving agricultural industry, can't support all of Israel's economic needs. You can't grow a country or reverse a negative foreign trade balance on an economic diet of strawberries and pomegranates.

When Binyamin Netanyahu became Finance Minister in 2000 Israel began sweeping changes to jump-start economic growth; like privatizing government owned companies in banking, telecommunications and oil exploration. Even these major changes in government spending and private investment have not been enough to counter the economic hardships brought on by monstrous income taxes (up to 60%), and the sharp decline of tourism and foreign investment due to the increase in Palestinian terrorism.

Like every other modern society, petroleum plays a major role in Israeli life. Since Israel imports virtually all of her oil, energy costs are expensive. According to a report in The Arutz Sheva Israel National News, the average Israeli family spends about 15% of their monthly income on fuel. Every dollar per barrel increase in the world's oil markets costs Israel $70 million in fuel costs per year.[1]

With Israeli oil consumption at 100 million barrels per year, a major oil discovery inside of its borders would have a huge economic impact. No other imaginable windfall on the magnitude of a major oil discovery exists in Israel today.

---

[1] "Oil Troubles in Israel", Arutz Sheva IsraelNationalNews.com, October 24, 2004

Geo-Political Situation

Israel would be safer if she were energy independent. Currently her oil needs are met at the pleasure of her outside suppliers. If anything in world politics were to prevent or discourage Israel's outside supply base the country would shut down in days. World oil politics is, to a great extent, controlled by OPEC. OPEC is controlled by the Arab nations. The threat Israel's Arab neighbors hold over her and the rest of the world is oil.

"If you upset us, we will turn off the oil spigot. If you comply with our wishes we will provide you with oil."

Using world oil supply as a political weapon, with Israel in the cross-hairs, the Arabs have tried to use their influence to slow Israel's foreign oil flow to a trickle.

As a part of the Camp David Peace accords the U.S. guaranteed Israel access to crude oil imports, but its ability to make good on that promise in the event of a crisis is questionable. In the event of another world oil crisis, Israel could very well be on her own.

A major oil discovery in Israel wouldn't make the world stop buying oil from the Arabs and start buying it from Israel. No huge relationship change with the US or European countries would bloom overnight. Deals have been made and infrastructures are already in place for oil supply to the developed world.

But for Israel, it would spell economic security and political safety. Israel's oil independence would fulfill the prophecy in the Old Testament book of Deuteronomy, "Israel then shall dwell in safety, alone" (33:28).

Energy

Israel's energy comes from oil, natural gas, coal and solar. Of these energy sources all but solar rely on foreign imports. Coal accounts for most of Israel's electrical power generation fuel and satisfies about 17% of Israel's overall power consumption. Israel doesn't produce any coal; her entire supply is imported from Australia, South Africa, and Britain.

Today natural gas is the bright spot in Israel's energy future. Significant quantities of natural gas from offshore fields will make an impact on electrical production and heavy industry. Because of this recently discovered source of energy existing oil fired electrical generation plants are being converted to burn cheap domestic natural gas rather than expensive imported oil.

Ashdod was the first power generation plant set up to produce electricity fueled solely from natural gas, piped in from the gas fields off the Mediterranean coast near Ashkelon. All of Israel's oil fired electrical generation plants are following suit. In the north, the Atlit gas pipeline infrastructure is being installed now to power the Carmel electrical generation plant. By 2010 more than 40% of all electricity in Israel will be produced by natural gas burning turbines.

Israel has been the world leader in solar energy technology development. More than 80% of Israel's hot water comes from solar and all new home construction in the country is required to include solar hot water systems. A 100 mega-watt solar power generation station is planned for "sometime in the future" in the Negev Desert, but the hopes of solar technology making a practical impact beyond hot water is doubtful.

Currently Israel consumes close to 300 thousand barrels of oil per day; about 72% of Israel's total energy consumption. Israel produces about 100 barrels of oil per day. To date Israel has produced about 18 million barrels of crude oil and the existing oil wells are about tapped out.

Compared to the amount of oil she uses, it is safe to say current domestic oil production is non-existent. Israel imports virtually all of her oil from the former Soviet Republics, Mexico and Egypt.

Even with her miserable success in trying to find oil domestically, Israel encourages oil and gas exploration. The Israeli government energy effort, however, runs on a shoestring. About $250 million between 1975 and 1985 was spent in Israeli oil exploration, most of it from foreign investment.

The government has privatized its oil companies, relying on outside investors to be the backbone of the country's oil and gas exploration efforts. The government negotiates exploration contracts and, as part of the deal shares access to all research and exploration data. At the expiration of the exploration contract this and any additional data, produced at the expense of foreign investors, is offered to new outside investors as Israel's contribution to further exploration efforts.

When it comes to oil and gas exploration, the government of Israel has done a good job of getting a lot from outsiders with very little invested from the inside. To date almost all exploration costs have been paid by private companies. Israel shares in all of the exploration data and a portion of any potential profits, and can at her discretion redirect all production to domestic needs.

In spite of the poor results a significant level of exploration has been accomplished. Over 420 exploration wells have been drilled and a good portion of the country is currently under some formed of exploration permit, license or lease.

The map on the next page shows wells drilled in Israel's short history and areas currently under permit, license or lease.

Ministry of National Infrastructures   State of Israel   Oil and Gas Section

Petroleum Rights
Updated January 01, 2005

Any offshore area not under
valid lease, license or permit
is currently closed for
petroleum exploration

Scale 1:1,250,000

LEGEND

Lease

License

Permit

Vertically
divided rights

Wells

Processed and produced by A. Varshavsky

Problems

One of the significant problems in Israel's oil exploration efforts is that big oil companies, known as the *"Majors"* shy away from any public business dealings with the state of Israel due to their ongoing relationships with Arab countries. The Arab oil producing nations have made it clear to international companies that any business dealings with Israel would mean an automatic boycott from them. The *"Majors"* simply have too much invested in Arab oil production to risk disfavoring their suppliers by showing any business interest in Israel.

This threat of boycott has left the field in Israel open to small, independent oil exploration companies. The problem with the small independents is that they don't have the budget for extended exploration. Because of limited funds, exploration projects (and companies) often dry up with the first dry hole; and in the oil exploration business there are a lot of dry holes.

Israel's difficult geology is another problem. According to seismic studies, the oil is deep and there are several problematic strata between the surface and potential reserves. Small independent companies with limited resources can risk going broke if they encounter extended drilling problems. Small independents often feel that they're better off simply putting their resources in other cheaper and easier to reach prospects.

The Israeli government has done little direct investment in finding oil domestically. They welcome outsiders who can pay their own way, but any exploration cost ends up being the responsibility of the outside investor. From Israel's perspective this is a fine approach; they enjoy the exploration efforts and possible future rewards at very little or no direct cost to the government. Unfortunately, the strategy of getting something for nothing hasn't produced significant oil deposits and it has a few problems that need to be considered:

1. The Majors aren't interested (at least publicly). The world's big oil companies have the best chance for long term oil exploration success. If committed to a project, they have the financial ability to continue operations beyond a single dry hole or extended drilling difficulties.

2. The small independent oil exploration companies lack the financial staying power in the event of dry holes or drilling problems. They also may lack the technical depth and production capability to follow through once a decent prospect has been identified.

3. Incentive. The majors have no incentive to explore for oil in Israel. The bulk of their investments and profits are tied up in countries that are antagonistic toward Israel or anyone who befriends her. Why should they risk their current business in known terrain for potential future business in potentially difficult terrain? The small independents, for the most part, would rather invest their limited financial resources closer to home and in easier terrain. For a small independent in Houston, Texas there are prospects closer to home than Israel that can be tapped at lower initial cost.

Stakeholders

There are three distinct groups that should be interested in the future of Israel's domestic oil supply. Regarding investment, these three groups should have an incentive that reaches beyond the current quarter's company balance sheet:

1. **Israelis** – Domestic energy resources are of life and death importance to the people of Israel. Reliance on foreign oil currently strangles Israel's economy and endangers her security. Domestic oil production equal to or greater than

domestic consumption would create a financial boom greater than anything in Israel's history. The discovery of significant oil reserves would have far greater economic impact than any other potential industry boom on Israel's horizon, including tourism, high tech, and the diamond cutting industries combined.

Energy self-sufficiency for Israel would defang her Arab enemies ... period. Foreign policy depends on oil. This is true of Israel, the U.S. and every other country on the globe. Decisions affecting every aspect of what one country does for, or to, another country are tainted by oil.

Israel's foreign policy is held on a leash by the U. S and other countries partly because on her need for foreign oil. If anyone believes U.S. foreign policy isn't influenced by world oil supply he should become a better student of world political events over the last thirty years. Foreign policy, free from the need of foreign oil supply would change the face of Israel's status in the world, both among her friends and enemies.

2. **Jews** – Jews around the world have been a primary source of aid for the State of Israel since her birth on May 14, 1948. The world's Jewish community supplies Israel with immigrants to fill the country's human resource needs, and provides financial resources in the form of charitable giving, direct business investment, technology, and tourism. Jews around the world are connected to Israel and are intensely interested in her health and survival in the future. The world's Jewish community should be profoundly interested in Israel's oil independence.

3. **Christians** – Jews don't necessarily claim Christians as spiritual brothers. Christians do, however, claim Jews. Christians believe that the Jews are God's chosen people. According to the analogy of an olive tree in the New Testament book of Romans, Israel is the true root and Gentile Christians are grafted in shoots from a wild olive.

> If some branches have been broken off, and you, though a
> wild olive shoot, have been grafted in among the others
> and now share in the nourishing sap from the olive root,
> do not boast over those branches. If you do, consider this:
> You do not support the root, but the root supports you.
>
> (Romans 11:17-18 NIV)

Israel is the political extension of the Jewish people.
As an independent state she represents the Jews as a people.
Christians should be interested in the health and survival of
Israel to the extent they identify with the Jews as God's
chosen people.

The Israeli Perspective

The Israelis, forced to be warriors from their birth, are
a people who truly desire peace. Surrounded by enemies, they
defend themselves and wish for a peace with neighbors that
know only conflict. A man I met in Israel recently showed us
the country's historical treasures and recent accomplishments.
Proud of his people and their accomplishment of building a
thriving country from a wilderness in just fifty years, he spoke
of future possibilities that today are still a dream. As we
traveled through Israel's lush northern countryside he mused
aloud:

> If only we could reach a peace with our neighbors, we
> could prosper together. First we would plant trees, and
> forests could grow in the desert of our neighbors as they
> do now in Israel. We could make fertile ground in the
> desert in just a few years, as we've done in Israel.

For a man who was born into war, whose parents
survived Hitler's holocaust death camps, who as a child
learned how to run from the school bus to the shelter of rock
outcroppings when the Syrian shells rained down from the

Golan Heights, I heard a dream of peace. What I didn't hear in his dialogue was hatred. I didn't hear forgiveness or forgetfulness, but neither did I hear hatred. Whether peace between Arab and Jew is possible only God knows. That Israelis deeply desire to live in peace is evident in their eyes, in their language, and in their dreams for the country.

Jews and Christians

Israeli Jews view American evangelical Christians with skepticism. They are suspicious of evangelical Christian motives; believing them to have their own agenda. Most Israeli Jews believe Christians' interest in Israel is to either proselytize the people (convert Jews to Christianity) or to bring about the battle of Armageddon in order to usher in the return of the Messiah. Incredibly, a popular belief among some Jews is that Christians are helping Israel in order to get the world's Jewish population back to the Holy Land so that they may be killed in the battle of Armageddon. Christians I've shared this with are shocked at the misconception, so far from their beliefs.

Many religious Jewish Zionists are open to aid from American evangelical Christians because of the shared belief that all of Israel (including Gaza and the West Bank) rightfully belongs to the Jews. Jewish Zionists, however, see assistance from American Christians as a marriage of convenience. They are not tickled over their new found allies in the struggle for their homeland, but beggars can't be choosers and American evangelical Christians seem to be the only non-Jewish friends to come forward.

American evangelical Christians do have their own agenda; and it's not to round up the world's Jews for the last battle. American evangelicals believe that the Jews, particularly Jews in Israel will be saved physically and spiritually in the last days.

Most Zionist Jews look sideways at Gentiles, even those trying to help. The belief that Christians have their own motives for their apparent friendship has been demonstrated, to the injury of Jews, throughout history. Among Jews, however, there exists the concept of a "righteous Gentile." These are Gentiles who truly seek to help the Jews without any ulterior motives.

In Israel's history, Lord Wingate (Wingate Center) and Lawrence Oliphant (Scottish writer) are examples of "righteous Gentiles." According to Israeli attorney Philip Mandelker, John Brown of Zion Oil & Gas is a "righteous Gentile." He may not be the only Christian oil prospector to be regarded so highly by Israelis, but the list of "righteous Gentiles" isn't a long one.

The core difference between religious Jews and evangelical Christians is that the Jews do not believe that Jesus Christ was and is the Messiah. Jews are waiting for the Messiah to come. Christians are waiting for the Messiah to return.

Mendy Gunda, an Israeli friend and tour guide illustrates this difference of opinion with a joke for his Christian clientele. "What's the first question a Jew will ask the Messiah when he comes?" The answer: "Is this your first visit to the Holy Land?"

The idea of the coming Messiah, however, is very real in the hearts of Zionist Jews. Jewish settlers in the Palestinian Gaza Strip were relocated to Israeli land as a condition of the "Roadmap to Peace." When interviewed, one Zionist settler who lost his home in the Gaza community his people built was philosophic in his larger view of the situation, "The train is going into a tunnel …. But it is moving forward. Every day brings us closer to the days of the Messiah."[2]

---

[2] "Settlers Ignore Gaza Countdown", Chicago Tribune April 22, 2005

The Christian Perspective

There are two reasons for evangelical Christians to be pro-Israel. The first is that evangelical Christians believe the Jews are God's chosen people. Israel is the God promised homeland of the Jews. Honoring, defending, and supporting Israel, from a Christian perspective, honors God.

According to the New Testament Gentile Christians are "grafted in" to God's family, like adopted children. The Jews (Israel) are God's chosen people or "chosen children." Gentile Christians believe that God's chosen people, whether they accept Jesus as Messiah or not, are to be held in special regard.

The Bible also teaches that in the end times (the period just before Christ returns to establish his kingdom on earth) that Israel will return to her land and prosper. Ultimately the Messiah will return and Israel will be saved physically and spiritually as a part of Christ's reign on earth and of his eternal kingdom.

The Arab Perspective

In their view, Arabs have received the short end of the stick from the Jews since the day they were born. Abraham, the father of the both Ishmael (from whom the Arabs descend) and Isaac (from whom the Jews descend) forsook tradition by giving Ishmael's rights and blessing as first born son to Isaac. Isaac's oldest son Esau also lost out at the hands of his younger brother Jacob. By bribes and treachery, Jacob stole Esau's birthright and blessing. Esau moved south, bereft of his blessing as first-born, to the desert eventually named "Edom" (Esau and Edom both mean "red").

The Arab nations descend from Ishmael and Esau. The Jews descend from Isaac and Jacob (Israel). From the Arab perspective, Jews have been cheating Arabs out of their birthright and blessing since the beginning.

177

God's perspective, however, prevails in the long run. He chooses whom he chooses, regardless of who was first-born. God doesn't answer to man. In choosing Isaac and Jacob, however, He did not completely bankrupt Ishmael and Esau. God remembered the complaint of Ishmael's mother Hagar and promised,

> And as for Ishmael, I have heard: Behold, I have blessed him, and will make him fruitful, and will multiply him exceedingly; twelve princes shall he beget, and I will make him a great nation.

(Genesis 17:20)

Esau didn't escape God's blessing either. When he complained to his father Isaac that little brother Jacob had stolen the blessing rightly belonging to him, Isaac produced an additional blessing for Esau,

> ...Behold, thy dwelling shall be the fatness of the earth, and of the dew of heaven from above; And by thy sword shalt thou live, and shalt serve thy brother; and it shall come to pass when thou shalt have the dominion, that thou shalt break his yoke from off thy neck.

(Genesis 27:39-40)

Esau founded Edom; today the country of Saudi Arabia. The word "fatness" in Esau's blessing above is the same ancient Hebrew word for oil. The promise that, "thy dwelling shall be the fatness (oil) of the earth" has been abundantly fulfilled in present day Saudi Arabia.

God didn't neglect His promises of nationhood and dominion to Ishmael and Esau. From the 5th century AD, when the religion of Islam was establish to today the Arab nations have had nearly complete control of the Middle East. Arab nations today control about 99% of the land mass in the Middle East and most of the world's proven oil reserves.

With all of this, they still hold a powerful grudge against the children of Isaac and Jacob. Their hatred for the people of Israel is endemic. The Arab world sees Israel as a usurper; a nation that occupies territory rightly belonging to the sons of Ishmael and Esau. The sworn oath to "drive Israel into the sea" is their single cure for this four thousand year old resentment. Only then, will they feel that ancient wrongs have been put right.

News of a vast oil reserve discovered in the land of Israel would infuriate the Arab world for several reasons. Firstly, since Israelis are regarded as trespassers and usurpers, any oil found in Israel would be viewed as the property of the Arab world by ancient right. The people of Israel benefiting from oil found in the land of Israel (which Arabs believe rightly belongs to them) is equivalent to Israelis stealing Arab oil.

Secondly, Arab legitimacy in the modern world comes from oil. Arabs enjoy their current level of importance and regard in the world because of their oil reserves. This may not be a popular statement but it's a true one. Israel, their birth enemy, suddenly becoming oil rich would insult the Arab world as a blow to their single source of status among the nations.

Thirdly, oil independence would make Israel stronger; economically and militarily. The idea of an economically and militarily strong Israel flies in the face of Arab domination in the region. A weak enemy is better than a strong one any day. Israel's Arab enemies have been pitifully inefficient in destroying her in the last fifty years; chances for an Arab victory in the future would be greatly diminished if Israel were energy self-sufficient and economically secure.

Fourthly, Israel having sufficient production to export oil could significantly reduce the cartel power OPEC enjoys today. To Arabs, the idea of Israel exporting oil is even more heinous than her oil self-sufficiency.

Not Enemies (sort of)

Not every Arab nation is sworn enemies with Israel. As a result of a February 2005 Mid-East Peace Summit Jordan and Egypt have reestablished diplomatic relations with Israel. This warming came as a result of the renewed promise of peace between Israel and the Palestinians. Egypt and Jordan are currently the only two Arab countries having peace treaties with Israel, but it is a cold peace.

Turkey is another exception. Although not Arab, Turkey is a Moslem country, throughout Israel's fifty year history Turkey has, to a great extent, maintained positive diplomatic relations.

The Boycott

The Arab boycott of Israel has been a part of its history since the country's birth in 1948. The Arab League (council of Arab nations) officially boycotted Israel; refusing to do business with Israel or any third country firms that have business dealings with Israel. The Arab countries know that they can use their oil trade with third parties as a powerful economic weapon against Israel. In 1978 the U.S. passed a law forbidding any U.S. company from participating with or agreeing to the boycott; but many other countries complied with Arab demands.

In spite of UN restrictions in Iraq's "Oil for Food" program after the first Gulf War, Iraq continued to coerce foreign business partners into the boycott. In 2004 U.S. investigators obtained copies of Iraqi contracts with Russian and Egyptian food and medicine suppliers pledging not to do business with Israel or ship product to Iraq through Israel. The Iraqi contract reinforces this pledge.

We hereby confirm our commitment and pledge not to deal with Israel. So that in the event of any infringement of this condition the Iraqi party will definitely cancel the contract and stop any future dealing with our firm.[3]

Most European countries have drafted laws against this kind of discrimination; but for some, their *business is business* mentality creates paths around anti-discrimination laws. France, who conducted considerable business with Iraq and today trades heavily with other Arab nations, has negotiated *boycott* language into their contracts, seemingly complying with the Arab boycott and European law.

The Moslem World

The Arab world is overwhelmingly Moslem. That is, the religion of the Arab world is Islam; so much so that the terms "Arab World" and "Moslem World" are often used in conversation interchangeably. The Moslem world encompasses more than Arab countries, but the Arab nations are the controlling entities in the world of Islam. Muslim's, almost completely, share the Arabs' hostility toward the Jews.

Iran's (Persian, not Arab) Ayatollah Ali Khamenei did his bit for the continued hatred of Israel and the U.S. by proposing a new Middle East oil policy to a crowd of his countrymen while they chanted "Death to Israel and America."[4]

His idea for Middle East oil policy was simple, "The oil belongs to the (Muslim) people and can be used as a weapon against the West and those who support the Savage regime of Israel." According to Ayatollah Khamenei's fundamentalist Muslim theology, Israel is the *Little Satan* and America is the *Big Satan*. If the world is to be set right, the

---

[3] "Baghdad Butcher's Oil Biz Slap at Israel", New York Post, October 16, 2004

[4] "Iranian Urges Muslims to Use Oil as a Weapon", New York Times, April 6, 2002

followers of Allah need to rid it of both *Satan* twins. Peace in the Middle East, as far as the fundamentalist Moslem world is concerned, involves the destruction and eradication of the State of Israel.

The Saudis, viewed as moderates and friends of the U.S., killed Ayatollah Khamenei's proposal to turn off the oil supply. However, Saudi Arabia, the world's largest oil producer and exporter and the most powerful voice in the Arab nations is in a tenuous position. OPEC's most powerful member is a one commodity economy. The commodity, of course is oil.

Even though Saudi Arabia has always played the part of moderate and friend of U.S. policy in the Arab world, its autocratic rulers continually walk the tight rope between their Western customers and their increasing anti-West population. For all the oil money injected into it, the Saudi economy is anything but robust. Unemployment is high and the jobs that do exist are usually dead-end bureaucratic busywork. The young Saudi population is being wooed heavily by Moslem fundamentalists encouraging a break with the West. Any change in the Saudi's standard of living stemming from less demand or lower prices for its only source of income could tip the scales in favor of the radical population. The next time radical fundamentalist Moslem leaders demand an end to Western oil supply, the Saudi's may not be able to prevent the idea from becoming reality.

The Palestinian Problem

Invisible, would be an apt description for the Arab Oil States in the latest attempts to ensure a lasting peace between Israel and the Palestinians. They've been invisible in the peace process, but not invisible altogether.

Iran is the major financer of Palestinian terrorism and the Arab States have never explicitly said that peace between

Israel and the Palestinians would be a good thing. Secretly (or not so secretly) they look forward to continued conflict in the area, hoping it will lead to the eventual downfall of the Jewish state. If the millions of dollars pumped into the Palestinian terror network by Iran and other Arab States were given to assist the Palestinians in building homes, schools and businesses rather than destroy both Palestinian and Jewish lives, the possibility of a Palestinian State becoming a reality would be much greater today.

The Palestinian Perspective

The Palestinian State is to be the independent homeland for Arab people living in the land of Palestine prior to the founding of the nation of Israel. The "Palestinian Authority" was set up as a pre-Palestine governing body; gaining status to "independent country," the world hoped, by 2005.

The birth of the Palestinian State is not on track. The current plan for Middle East peace, put together by the U.S., the European Union, Russia, and the U.N., called the "Road Map" to peace is to be achieved in phases, ultimately leading to an independent Palestinian State. Israel and the Palestinian Authority are still in phase one; and it isn't going well.

In Phase One of the plan, Palestinians are supposed to halt all terror activities. Since the "Road Map" was laid out, terrorist attacks have increased, not halted or even decreased. With the death of Yasser Arafat, in many eyes the primary nurturer of Palestinian terrorism, hope sprang up for a Palestinian effort at the peace plan. Israel, as their part in the peace process was to stop building settlements in Palestinian territories and begin dismantling existing settlements.

Israeli settlement building inside Palestinian territory has increased since the peace plan was laid out. In spite of pulling Israeli settlers out of the Gaza Strip (Palestinian

183

territory), settlement building in the Palestinian West Bank has continued as scheduled.

The "Road Map" has hit a road block. Neither side will engage in Phase One without proof that the other is simultaneously fulfilling their half of the bargain. Neither side is making promises that they will comply, whether the other side fulfills their end or not. From whoever's perspective it's viewed, the Israeli/Palestinian "Road Map" to peace has taken a detour.

Palestinian terrorism continues to increase in spite of the attempted peace process. Incidents of attacks from terrorist groups went up in 2004 from the year before. Due to Israeli Defense Forces checkpoints and the disputed security wall between Israel and the West Bank, however, Israeli fatalities and injuries have gone down. Regardless of the political uproar the security wall and IDF checkpoints have caused, these two measures have saved Israeli civilian lives. An upswing in the relatively ineffective mortar and Kassam rocket attacks from inside Palestinian territory and the marked decrease of more deadly suicide bombings is proof that Israeli measures to limit terrorists access has been successful.

There is a school of thought that says if a vast oil deposit was discovered in the land that the resulting prosperity would lead to a lasting peace between Palestinians and Israel. The idea being that neither party could afford to be at war against the other with such a treasure at stake.

A peace between Palestinians and Israelis driven by mutual oil wealth sounds like a great idea. Unfortunately, the mutual animosity between the two parties isn't driven by who gets dibs over valuable mineral resources. The resource is the land itself. As long as Israel exists in the land, Palestinians, like their Arab brothers, will continue to regard the Jews as invaders.

The State of Israel, of course, isn't going anywhere. Not only is Israel committed to staying in the land rightfully apportioned to them by the League of Nations in 1947, many in Israel are committed to occupy the land rightly apportioned to them by God three thousand years ago. The land apportioned to them by God includes the Palestinian territory. Israel's former Prime Minister Ariel Sharon made no bones about it. Israel is not going to make any unilateral effort to ensure the reality of an independent Palestinian state.

The World's Perspective

Depending on which U.S. Government Department of Energy report you read, current world oil production is about 84 million barrels per day. Daily world oil consumption is 84 millions barrels, matching production. The world burns as much oil as it produces. Demand, however, is estimated to nearly double by the year 2025. Proven world oil reserves today are estimated at just over 1.3 trillion barrels. At the present growth rate of demand with the current proven reserves, the world's oil fields should be going dry in about twenty-five years.

Russia

As allies with the U S against Germany during World War II the Soviet Union was obligated to support the 1947 UN Partition of Palestine Resolution and recognize Israel as an independent State in 1948. The relationship between the U.S.SR and Israel declined rapidly after that. The Soviets soon changed allegiance and began backing Egypt and Syria in the Middle East. The Soviets were also among the first to begin supplying the PLO (Palestinian Liberation Organization) with military hardware to use against Israel.

In the mid-1980's the Soviets tried a warming tactic in an effort to counter-balance the strong U.S relationship with Israel and to be seen as a *player* in the Middle-East peace process. They hosted their own *"peace summit"* in Helsinki in an effort to re-establish relations with Israel. Part of the deal they were seeking was increased access to Israel, both in diplomatic (spy) venues and travel of Soviet citizens to Israel. They were also interested in Soviet property in Israel, namely that of the Russian Orthodox Church.

Table 3. World Oil Reserves by Country as of January 1, 2007

Country	Oil Reserves (Billion Barrels)
Saudi Arabia	262.3
Canada	179.2
Iran.	136.3
Iraq.	115.0
Kuwait	101.5
United Arab Emirates.	97.8
Venezuela	80.0
Russia	60.0
Libya	41.5
Nigeria	36.2
Kazakhstan	30.0
United States	21.8
China	16.0
Qatar	15.2
Mexico	12.4
Algeria	12.3
Brazil	11.8
Angola	8.0
Norway.	7.8
Azerbaijan	7.0
Rest of World	65.5
World Total	**1,317.4**

"Worldwide Look at Reserves and Production," Oil & Gas Journal, Vol. 104, No. 47 (December 18, 2006), pp. 24-25.

Israel had its own interests in the apparent warm front coming down from Russia. The Soviets possessed two assets of great value to Israel. The USSR was home to a huge population of Jews and many of these Jews would immigrate to Israel if given the opportunity. Israel wanted a much freer immigration policy for Jews coming from Soviet States.

Another asset Israel couldn't turn down was oil. Soviet oil fields were pumping about 12 million barrels a day in 1986. Russian oil supply was fat, cheap and close to Israel. Despite its history of backing her enemies Israel saw the USSR as a promising source for her oil needs. Today Israel imports the majority of her oil from the former Soviet Union – Russia and the Caspian region (Kazakhstan, Turkmenistan, etc.).

Russia is determined to take a greater role in Israel's future. Other than the U.S., Russia is the only single country entity with an active role in the Israel/Palestinian "Road Map" to peace. Member powers of the "Quartet", the body responsible for creating and ensuring the "Road Map" peace plan include the U.S., Russia, the European Union, and the U.N. Russian president Vladimir Putin is stepping to the forefront by hosting "Quartet" meetings and the next Middle East peace conference in Moscow.

Russia has also pushed for a closer relationship with Israel in the areas of Israel's large Russian speaking population and anti-terrorism. With all its feints toward an Israeli/Palestinian peace Russia continues, however, to back the Palestinian cause and slander Israel through front organizations such as the World Peace Council.[5]

Russia and her former satellite states now supply Israel with 90% of its imported oil. If Israel were to suddenly discover reserves sufficient to become oil independent, the former Soviet States would lose a very important customer. If Israel were to stop buying oil, Russia's reasons for positive relations would diminish. With an increasing Moslem foothold in the former Soviet States, Russia could easily

---

[5] "Putin Due in Israel on Historic Visit", Associated Press, April 27, 2005

return to the side of *old friends* (war materiel customers) in the Middle East.

Current proven oil reserves in Russia and the former Soviet states are 97 billion barrels. Today these states produce about 12.5 million barrels per day. Following the expected increase in demand and assuming production will increase to meet demand, the former Soviet states should run out of oil by 2020.

Western Europe

As a group, Western Europe is pretty pragmatic when it comes to Israel. It doesn't carry the political hatred of the Arab world and it lacks any spiritual or cosmic reason to support Israel. Simply put, Europe wants what it wants for its own purposes and if working with Israel gets it what it wants, it's ready to be friends. If being friends with Israel prevents it from getting what it wants, then Israel is out of the picture and new friends (OPEC) are in.

Europe does have Jewish and Christian populations that are pro-Israel and Moslem populations that are pro-Arab; but neither group necessarily affects foreign policy. Recent Islamic terrorism, unfortunately, has managed to steer the ship of foreign policy in some

European countries. Europe's dual personality is born from and fueled by commercial interests. The region depends heavily on Arab oil and they will do nothing politically to upset that supply. Europe demonstrated during the days leading to the fall of Iraq that alienating Israel and the U.S. if necessary would not be too high a price to pay to preserve their established oil for "anything you want" contract with OPEC nations.

On the other hand, about forty percent of Israeli foreign trade, in the form of agricultural products and high-tech goes to Western Europe. Western Europe doesn't seem to be bound by moral or religious restrictions concerning the Arabs or the Israelis; just give them what they want and they'll put on the face required for the day.

An oil discovery in Israel sufficient for export to European markets may increase *warm feelings* toward Israel. On the other hand, Arab nations remain Europe's largest oil supplier. In the event of a major oil discovery in Israel it will be interesting to see where Europe finds its best deal and its closest ally.

China and the Far East

There is a dragon asleep in the backyard. She's been asleep for a long time, but now she is beginning to wake; and when she's awake and active the entire world will feel her hot breath on its neck. China is the largest single emerging market the world has ever seen.

Leading the pack of Asian countries, including India and South Korea, China and her neighbors combined currently consume about 75% of the energy consumed in North America (U.S., Canada, and Mexico) By 2025 China and her neighbors will consume nearly 30% more total energy than North America. Asia will feed her exploding energy requirements from some source. How, where, and what strings may be attached to Asia's oil supply are anyone's guess. One thing is certain, however, Asia, with China leading, will eclipse every other oil consumer in the world.

The U.S. Perspective

The U.S. imports nearly fourteen million barrels of oil per day; about sixty-six percent of its total consumption. Seventeen percent of that comes from the Persian Gulf.

According to Red Caveny,[6] the President and CEO of the American Petroleum institute, America's demand for energy will increase significantly over the next twenty years. Quoting Department of Energy forecasts in his State of the Energy Industry 2005 address he gives the numbers the U.S. can expect through 2025:

- Real GDP will increase by 95 percent

- Population will increase by 20 percent

- Total energy consumption will increase by 36 percent

- Petroleum demand will increase by 39 percent

- Natural gas demand will increase by 40 percent

- Coal demand will increase by 34 percent

- Electricity consumption will increase by 50 percent

Caveny went on to say that America's greatest energy problem was the lack of any comprehensive plan for the future. The net effect, according to Caveny, of the current U.S. energy policy is to decrease reliance on domestic sources and increase dependence of foreign imports. This means that over the next twenty years America's reliance on foreign oil will increase exponentially. Caveny goes on to say,

> We cannot discuss the challenge of meeting the growing U.S. energy demand without first understanding the global energy situation. In the world of energy, the U.S. must operate in a global market. What others do in that market matters greatly.

Israeli oil independence probably wouldn't have a profound effect on America's energy future. The U.S. is by far, the world's largest user and importer of oil. No single oil

---

[6] "State of the Energy Industry 2005, Petroleum Issues", American Petroleum Institute, January 18, 2005

exporting country, including Saudi Arabia, could supply U.S. consumption. At a rate twenty-one million barrels per day, U.S. consumption matches the total daily output from the Persian Gulf nations.

U.S foreign policy toward Israel addresses Israel's oil supply, not her potential surplus. For better or worse, current U.S. foreign policy ensures Israeli oil supply. The United States, in a 1975 "Memorandum of Understanding" with Israel, guaranteed the supply of Israel's oil needs in the event of a crisis, even if it means reducing America's oil supply.[7]

The U.S. and Israel have also signed an energy cooperation agreement in February of 2000 that promises teamwork in the areas of natural gas, coal, solar technology, and electrical generation.[8]

The U.S., however, learned its lesson during the first Arab oil embargo. Never again will it enact any foreign policy without first considering how the Arab world will react. The Arab world has become very much a part of America's foreign policy decision making. Between America's loyalties to Israel and its energy threat from the Arabs, it walks a tightrope, that falling from, wherever it landed would be devastating.

As far as American opinion regarding Israel and Middle East peace goes, it's as polarized as it's ever been. The internal political lines for or against support of Israel have been drawn in this country and the results show just how divided America has become regarding Israel.

In a May 17, 2001 letter to the editor titled *"Safer to Bomb Civilians"* in The Houston Chronicle Art Milstein

---

[7] "Israel's pipe dream: getting oil from Iraq." The St. Petersburg Times, August 15, 2004

[8] "Israel's ongoing foreign energy dependence." UPI Perspective, August 11, 2004

spoke for many Americans when he voiced his frustration over the conflict between Israelis and Palestinians.

Like any thinking person I'm appalled at what's happening in Gaza and the West Bank. I don't believe Ariel Sharon's visit caused it – it was too well organized and just waiting to happen.

And I feel disgusted by the world's media handling of the news. Rocks can kill and maim; are soldiers supposed to throw rocks back?

It's stupid to throw rocks and try to burn people who carry guns. Bombing a busload of civilians or a market is safer.

I feel for the plight of Palestinians: in 50 years, their Arab "brothers" have offered them only guns, not homes.

If Israel had oil, it would be safer. And don't be misled: When push comes to shove, the world will feel Jews are cheaper than oil. I wouldn't blame God if he gave up on us all.

CHAPTER FIFTEEN

SIGNIFICANCE

Ishmael, Isaac, Jacob and Esau

Ishmael and Isaac, in their day, saw their relative positions and destinies from their own unique individual and historic perspectives. Ishmael was Abraham's oldest son, born to him by Hagar, his wife's servant. By ancient custom the first born son deserved his father's blessing and birthright.

Isaac, Abraham's second son, born to him by his wife Sarah was God's promised child. By God's choice, Isaac was given the birthright and blessing, belonging by custom to Ishmael. This created an enmity between Ishmael and Isaac, but the idea that someday their descendents would be warring nations and the world's focus would rest on their petroleum reserves was outside of their comprehension - beyond their perspective.

Esau and Jacob, in their day, saw their relative positions and destinies from their unique individual and historic positions. Twins, sons of the same father and mother, born on the same day; their issues and circumstances were not the same as those of their father Isaac or uncle Ishmael. Esau and Jacob had their own destinies, as God prophesied to Rebekah their mother,

> ...Two nations are in thy womb, and two manner of people shall be separated from thy bowels; and the one

people shall be stronger than the other people; and the elder shall serve the younger.

(Genesis 25:23)

Esau the oldest, long on brawn and short on brain, traded his birthright to his twin brother Jacob for a bowl of stew. Later, when the boys were men and father Isaac was old and nearing death, Jacob bested his brother again by obtaining their father's blessing, reserved for the first-born, by deceit. Tricking his brother and father, Jacob, whose name literally means "grabber," had grabbed the birthright and blessing meant for Esau.

Jacob and Esau, like their father and uncle, viewed their circumstances from ground level. Like their father and uncle, that they would become the progenitors of warring nations and inheritors of the world's petroleum reserves was outside of their ability to comprehend – beyond their perspective.

Today this ancient family feud is about a lot more than sheep, goats, and the family tent. Ishmael, Isaac, Esau, and Jacob are now just names from history - dead forefathers. Nations have risen from men and petroleum oil has replaced olive oil as a universal commodity.

The old enmity between these brothers still exists but the stakes have gone up. Today Israel and the Arab nations, if not at open war, are at least circling in a wary detent.

The ongoing terror campaign waged against Israel is testimony that war, not peace, is always lying just beneath the surface. The sons of Jacob (Israel) are still called "grabbers" by their Arab relatives. The sons of Esau are still wanting their birthright and blessing back. Unfortunately, the perspective hasn't changed much. The sons of Jacob and Esau, Isaac and Ishmael, like their fathers, are only seeing the situation from ground level.

Perspective

Perspective is the view of an object relative to the position of the viewer. The closer the viewer is to an object the more restricted his view is of the entire object. As the viewer backs away his perspective widens so that he sees the object and the space surrounding it more clearly.

I have a large map of the world hanging on my office wall. If I place my nose on the map's surface, with Los Angeles as ground zero, my perspective of the map and the world is extremely limited. In fact I can't even see Los Angeles; everything's a blur. But as I back away from the wall my vision begins to clear. At six inches I can see Los Angeles and read the names of the surrounding cities I can even vaguely make out parts of Canada to the north, Mexico to the south and the blue of oceans on either side.

As I continue to back away from the wall the names of cities, states and provinces of North America come into focus. I see the oceans that border North America and in my peripheral vision I can see other continents where the oceans end.

From three feet the world comes into view; with North America in the center (thanks to Rand McNally). I can see Africa and Europe, Russia, Asia and Australia. I can see how the countries are situated within the continents, their relative proximity or distance from other nations.

At six feet I see the entire map at a glance. I see how Russia and China, sliced in half by the map's right border, continue on the left from where they were bisected. I can still read the names of the countries and continents printed on the map, but the cities are too small for me to make out.

By the latitudinal and longitudinal lines growing outward as they travel away from the equator I understand that the map displays distance in smaller increments close to the equator, increasing in size as it travels away north or south. This makes Greenland, in the far north appear slightly larger than South America in the center, even though South America is about nine times the size of Greenland. I remember that the earth is a globe, not flat like the map and that these growing distances are a cartographer's tool to display a round globe on a flat wall.

At this distance I can finally see the world for what it is and understand the map in its full view. I also realize that the map is not the only object in the room. In my periphery I can see my desk to the left and bookshelves to the right; beyond the desk I even catch a glimpse out my office window to the world outside.

By backing away from the map the big picture came into view. I gained perspective; first seeing Los Angeles, then North America, then the world, and finally the map itself. I realized that Los Angeles wasn't the only object on the map, nor was North America. It was a map of the entire world.

I also realized that the map was not the world, but just the mapmaker's depiction of the world. The mapmaker created the map to be viewed at a distance, so the viewer could see the world in perspective.

The Lesson

The lesson of the map is perspective – how we see things. Men can only view objects and circumstances from where they are. At ground level the world is a blur. As far as we're concerned, if anything does exist beyond our noses it's out of focus; our life is consumed with the daily struggle of personal existence.

Distance, in time and circumstance, brings a wider perspective. Once our immediate survival needs are satisfied, we can step back for a moment and see our situation from a little wider perspective. Time also adds to our perspective. Today we have the luxury of looking back over our history, learning from mistakes of the past and vowing not to repeat them.

The problem remains, however, that our perspective of the world is limited by our relative proximity to it, both in time and space. If we could somehow figuratively escape earth's orbit and the restrictions of time and space, perhaps then we could get the big picture; a true perspective of the world and our situation in it; perhaps even some cosmic mapmaker's purpose behind the whole thing.

The good news is that there is a map of our human situation and there is a mapmaker who can guide us as we navigate on life's oceans. God is the Mapmaker. His Word is a map and within its pages are the mapmaker's tools, laid into the map so that we can gain a true perspective of our place in the world.

The stories of Abraham, Ishmael, Isaac, Jacob, Esau and Joseph are part of the map of human history. From those stories we can gain perspective, not just of man's history in general, but of our own relative position in the world. This map, the Bible, is as relevant to the modern navigator as it was to those ancient sojourners whose lives became a part of the map, a part of the story. The Mapmaker included tools in the map to help us see our own situation in its proper perspective.

God doesn't see from man's perspective. God's perspective is from above. He's free from the limits of time and space. He's the Mapmaker. He sees the whole map; where it begins and where it ends.

God's interaction with Abraham, Sarah, Hagar, Ishmael and Isaac, came from a perspective that took into account circumstances that occurred millions of years before they were born and circumstances yet to occur, thousands of years after their deaths.

When He spoke to Rebekah as her two sons fought inside her womb, he knew the chain of events that led to their birth and the chain of events that would result from their birth.

Today, in the midst of Middle East conflict and the world's trepidation over future oil supply, God sees events, whether they occurred in the 16th century BC or the 21st century AD, from a perspective above that of man.

God's Purpose

God's perspective is tied to His purpose; and God is purposeful. The universe was created on purpose and as a part of God's purpose. This world and the race of men who inhabit it were created on purpose and as a part of God's purpose. When and how this world and its people reach the expiration of the current age and begin the next will be according to God's purpose.

God doesn't purpose man toward hate and killing and mutual destruction; but in the midst of the hate and killing God's purpose remains.

In His sovereignty, God chose Isaac and not Ishmael. He preferred Jacob to Esau. In his sovereign purpose, God named the children of Israel as His chosen people and gave them an inheritance in the land of Canaan. This land and all of its resources, above and below the ground, was given by God to Israel and his children as an "everlasting possession."

> Then Jacob (Israel) said to Joseph, God Almighty appeared to me at Luz in the land of Canaan and blessed me, and He said to me, "Behold, I will make you fruitful and numerous, and I will make you a company of peoples, and will give this land to your descendents after you for an everlasting possession.
>
> (Genesis 48:3 NASB)

Prophecy Fulfilled

Is the discovery of a vast oil reserve in the land of Israel really a fulfillment of end time prophecy? Jacob's blessing appears twice in the Old Testament, first from Jacob himself in the forty-ninth chapter of Genesis; then by Moses four hundred years later, in Deuteronomy thirty-three.

Jacob's blessing is the source of our clues regarding God's promise of oil in Israel. As a preamble to his blessing in Genesis, Jacob tells his sons, "... Gather yourselves together that I may tell you that which shall befall you in the last days" (49:1). The blessing described in Genesis 49 was meant for the descendents of Jacob's sons, not the sons themselves. It is a promise to his sons, not for the day it was given, but for the last days.

Does the passage in Deuteronomy in any way refer to the "last days"? Moses is restating Jacob's blessing to the descendents of Jacob's twelve sons. If Jacob meant his blessing for the last days when he first gave it to his sons, then Moses could have only meant the same when he restated the blessing to their descendents. Moses gives us some other clues that Jacob's blessing included his *last days* children.

Deuteronomy 32 is known as "The Song of Moses." It is a preamble to Jacob's blessing; the last time he was to address the Children of Israel. Verses eight and nine speak of a time long before their gathering on the borders of the Promised Land.

> When the Most High gave the nations their inheritance,
> When He separated the sons of man, He set the
> boundaries of the peoples According to the number of the
> sons of Israel... For the Lord's portion is his people;
> Jacob is the allotment of His inheritance. (NASB)

God's perspective sees way before and way ahead of the present moment. This passage refers to some time early on in earth's history. When Moses spoke of God "giving the nations their inheritance," "separating the sons of man" and "setting the boundaries of the people" he was not speaking in the context of his own day. This passage refers to a time in the remote past. But this only a passage referring to the "first days," let's look for something referring to the "last days."

Deuteronomy 33 contains Jacob's Blessing, given by Moses to the Children of Israel before entering the Promised Land. Verse 17 gives us the clue we are looking for. Speaking of Joseph, Moses prophecies:

> In majesty he is like a firstborn bull; his horns are the horns of a wild ox. With them he will gore the nations, even those at the ends of the earth. (NIV)

Joseph, upon whose head the blessing (oil) rests will be as a bull, whose horns will "gore the nations, even those at the ends of the earth." We know Moses couldn't have been speaking in the context of the day. The "nations at the ends of the earth" were way outside of the scope of the Israelite's conquest of Canaan. We also know that Joseph "goring the nations" isn't an event that has happened to date. This passage refers to something that is yet to take place.

Isn't it interesting that the Bible reveals that Jacob's blessing (oil) rests on the crown of the head of Joseph and Moses prophesies that the nations will be "gored" by the crown of the head of Joseph?

The End of Days

Biblical prophecy is fulfilled for God's purpose, in His time. But sometimes man, acting according to his own purposes, plays a role. Pursuing his own purpose and power man has, n the past, set the scene for God's purpose.

A good example is in the Old Testament story of the Pharaoh refusing to release the Children of Israel from Egypt. God's purpose was that the Children of Israel should leave their captivity in Egypt and move into the Promised Land of Canaan.

If the Pharaoh had listened to God's spokesman, Moses, in the beginning and simply released the Children of Israel from bondage, God's purpose *seemingly* would have been fulfilled. But that wasn't God's full purpose. His purpose was to prove to the nations, beyond a shadow of a doubt, that He was divine and He was in charge.

Pharaoh would finally relent and free the Children of Israel. But not until ten plagues had been visited on the people of Egypt. Pharaoh repented after each plague and reneged on his promise each time. Finally, as a result of the tenth plague, the death of every first born male of Egypt, including Pharaoh's own son, he agreed to release the Children of Israel from slavery.

The Egyptians were so defeated by the plagues and relieved at the Israelites departure that they loaded them with all the wealth of Egypt as they departed.

After a few days Pharaoh began to regret his decision. The Egyptian economy would quickly disintegrate without the slave labor provided by the Children of Israel. Pharaoh mounted his army in full pursuit to overtake and capture his former workforce and return them to Egypt.

God again miraculously delivered the Children of Israel by opening a dry path in the Red Sea providing the Children of Israel an avenue of escape from the armies of Pharaoh, then closing it again drowning Pharaoh and his pursuing armies.

God purposed Pharaoh to act in his own interest. God hardened Pharaoh's heart against Moses and the Children of Israel in order that by Pharaoh's actions, God's divine power and would be revealed for God's glory. Romans 9:17–18 summarizes God's purpose in Pharaoh's actions:

> For the Scripture says to Pharaoh: "I raised you up for this very purpose, that I might display my power in you and that my name might be proclaimed in all the earth." Therefore God has mercy on whom he wants to have mercy, and he hardens whom he wants to harden. (NIV)

Gog and Magog

We learned in Chapter Eight that Russia (Gog and Magog) would be drawn down into Israel to take a "spoil." As it was for Pharaoh in the days of Moses, so shall it be for Gog and Magog in the last days.

The Old Testament book of Ezekiel predicts that Gog and Magog along with Persia (Iran), Ethiopia, Libya, Gomer (Germany), and Togarmah (Turkey) will be drawn down into Israel. Most of the southern Russian Republics are Islamic. Iran, Ethiopia, Libya, and Turkey are Islamic nations. We can assume that the balance of Arab/Islamic world, with their long standing enmity toward Israel, will join in the fray.

> After many days you will be called to arms. In future years you will invade a land that has recovered from war, whose people were gathered from many nations to the mountains of Israel, which had long been desolate. They had been brought out from the nations, and now all of them live in safety. You and all your troops and the many nations with you will go up, advancing like a storm; you will be like a cloud covering the land.

> This is what the Sovereign LORD says: "On that day thoughts will come into your mind and you will devise an evil scheme. You will say, 'I will invade a land of unwalled villages; I will attack a peaceful and unsuspecting people—all of them living without walls and without gates and bars. I will plunder and loot and turn my hand against the resettled ruins and the people

gathered from the nations, rich in livestock and goods, living at the center of the land.'"

(Ezekiel Chapter 38: 8-12 NIV)

These countries will invade a land that is at peace and living in safety. They will have "devised an evil scheme" to plunder the Nation of Israel. Russia and her allies will invade Israel for their own purposes, to plunder the land; but, like Pharaoh, it is God's purpose that will direct the action.

Earlier in Chapter 38 of Ezekiel, God states, "… I am against you, O Gog … I will turn you around, put hooks in your jaws and bring you out with your whole army …." (Vs.3 – 4 NIV).

God orchestrates even the evil intentions of man to His purpose. Like Pharaoh, God's purpose for Gog and his allies is to reveal Himself to the nations.

> In the days to come, O Gog, I will bring you against my land, so that the nations may know me when I show myself holy through you before their eyes.

(Ezekiel 38:16 NIV)

What happens when Gog and his allies invade Israel? Just like the pursuing armies of Pharaoh, they will be miraculously destroyed.

> I will turn you around and drag you along. I will bring you from the far north and send you against the mountains of Israel. Then I will strike your bow from your left hand and make your arrows drop from your right hand. On the mountains of Israel you will fall, you and all your troops and the nations with you. I will give you as food to all kinds of carrion birds and to the wild animals. You will fall in the open field, for I have spoken, declares the Sovereign LORD. I will send fire on Magog and on those who live in safety in the coastlands, and they will know that I am the LORD.

(Ezekiel 38: 2-6 NIV)

The End Game

What is God's final purpose? Why would He pit nation against nation? What possible reason could He have for promising Jacob's sons a vast oil reserve, only to be discovered in the last days? Why involve Russia?

God's final purpose is his first purpose. His beginning game is the same as His end game.

> And so I will show my greatness and my holiness, and I will make myself known in the sight of many nations. Then they will know that I am the Lord.
>
> (Ezekiel 38:23)
>
> I will make known my holy name among my people Israel. I will no longer let my holy name be profaned, and the nations will know that I the LORD am the Holy One in Israel.
>
> (Ezekiel 39:7 NIV)

What about the nation of Israel? Does God have a purpose for modern day Israel? Will it be destroyed by its own blessing? Will Russia and her allies invade Israel to destroy her and take her oil in the last days?

Ezekiel 39 tells us that just the opposite will happen. God will destroy the armies of Gog and Magog and not only will Israel be saved, they will be redeemed.

Don't lose sight - God's final purpose is his original purpose. His purpose from the beginning was and is to reveal Himself first and foremost to His chosen people Israel, then to the nations.

> From that day forward the house of Israel will know that I am the LORD their God. And the nations will know that the people of Israel went into exile for their sin, because they were unfaithful to me. So I hid my face from them and handed them over to their enemies, and they all fell

by the sword. I dealt with them according to their uncleanness and their offenses, and I hid my face from them.

Therefore this is what the Sovereign LORD says: I will now bring Jacob back from captivity and will have compassion on all the people of Israel, and I will be zealous for my holy name. They will forget their shame and all the unfaithfulness they showed toward me when they lived in safety in their land with no one to make them afraid. When I have brought them back from the nations and have gathered them from the countries of their enemies, I will show myself holy through them in the sight of many nations. Then they will know that I am the LORD their God, for though I sent them into exile among the nations, I will gather them to their own land, not leaving any behind. I will no longer hide my face from them, for I will pour out my Spirit on the house of Israel, declares the Sovereign LORD.

(Ezekiel 39:22-29)

APPENDICES

SPIRITUAL HELP

Are you looking for answers? Here you will find direction and encouragement for your pursuit of the Way, the Truth, and the Life.

How to Become a Christian

The central theme of the Bible is God's love for you and for all people. This love was revealed when Jesus Christ, the Son of God, came into the world as a human being, lived a sinless life, died on the cross, and rose from the dead. Because Christ died, your sins can be forgiven, and because He conquered death you can have eternal life. You can know for sure what will become of you after you die.

You have probably heard the story of God's love referred to as the "Gospel." The word Gospel simply means "Good News." The Gospel is the Good News that, because of what Christ has done, we can be forgiven and can live forever.

But this gift of forgiveness and eternal life cannot be yours unless you willingly accept it. God requires an individual response from you. The following verses from the Bible show God's part and yours in this process:

God's Love Is Revealed in the Bible

"For God so loved the world that he gave his one and only Son, that whoever believes in him shall not perish but have eternal life." —— John 3:16 (NIV)

God loves you. He wants to bless your life and make it full and complete. And He wants to give you a life which will last forever, even after you experience physical death.

We Are Sinful

"For all have sinned and fall short of the glory of God." — Romans

3:23 (NIV)

You may have heard someone say, "I'm only human— nobody's perfect." This Bible verse says the same thing: We are all sinners. We all do things that we know are wrong. And that's why we feel estranged from God—because God is holy and good, and we are not.

Sin Has a Penalty

"For the wages of sin is death." —Romans 6:23 (NIV)

Just as criminals must pay the penalty for their crimes, sinners must pay the penalty for their sins. If you continue to sin, you will pay the penalty of spiritual death: You will not only die physically; you will also be separated from our holy God for all eternity. The Bible teaches that those who choose to remain separated from God will spend eternity in a place called hell.

Christ Has Paid Our Penalty!

"But God demonstrates his own love for us in this: While we were still sinners, Christ died for us." —Romans 5:8 (NIV)

The Bible teaches that Jesus Christ, the sinless Son of God, has paid the penalty for all your sins. You may think you have to lead a good life and do good deeds before God will love you. But the Bible says that Christ loved you enough to die for you, even when you were rebelling against Him.

Salvation Is a Free Gift

"For it is by grace you have been saved, through faith—and this not from yourselves, it is the gift of God—not by works, so that no one can boast." —Ephesians 2:8-9 (NIV)

The word grace means "undeserved favor." It means God is offering you something you could never provide for yourself: forgiveness of sins and eternal life, God's gift to you is free. You do not have to work for a gift. All you have to do is joyfully receive it, Believe with all your heart that Jesus Christ died for you!

Christ Is at Your Heart's Door

"Here I am! I stand at the door and knock. If anyone hears my voice and opens the door, I will come in and eat with him, and he with me."

—Revelation 3:20 (NIV)

Jesus Christ wants to have a personal relationship with you. Picture, if you will, Jesus Christ standing at the door of your heart (the door of your emotions, intellect and will). Invite Him in; He is waiting for you to receive Him into your heart and life.

You Must Receive Him

"Yet to all who received him, to those who believed in his name, he gave the right to become children of God." —John 1:12 (NIV)

When you receive Christ into your heart you become a child of God, and have the privilege of talking to Him in prayer at any time about anything. The Christian life is a personal relationship to God through Jesus Christ. And best of all, it is a relationship that will last for all eternity.

Taken from "Your Christian Life" 1965, 1968, as "Aids to Christian Living," 1986 as "Practical Steps in Christian Living," 1995 as "Beginning Your Christian Life," 1997 as "Your Christian Life," Billy Graham Evangelistic Association.

Appendix B

Zion Oil & Gas Vision Book

THE OIL OF IS'RA-EL

"Write the vision; make it plain upon tablets, so he may run who reads it. For still the vision awaits its time; it hastens to end - it will not lie. If it seems slow, wait for it; it will surely come, it will not delay"

– Habakkuk 2: 2&3

FOUNDER'S TESTIMONY
THE VISION AND THE CALLING

Dear Friends,

When first visiting Israel in 1983, I believe G-d gave me a scripture (I Kings 8:41-43), a vision (Oil for Israel) and, as a Christian Zionist and New Covenant believer (Isaiah 65:1), the calling to render assistance to the Jewish people and Nation of Israel and to aid them in the Restoration of the Land by providing the oil and gas necessary to help the People of Israel maintain their political and economic independence. (Leviticus 19:33, 34) (Exodus 6:6-8)

In the Bible, G-d sovereignty declares that Israel is His chosen people (Exodus 4:22); and we can gain some understanding of G-d's choice, His vision and purpose by reading (Deuteronomy 7).

As a Christian Zionist, I declare "thy people shall be my people, and thy God my God" (Ruth 1:16); and, I believe that , as true Christians, we must all so identify with Israel, as we are all part of the "wild olive branch" grafted onto the olive tree by the grace of G-d (Romans 11). Moreover, I identify with Israel because I share in their struggle and understand a little something of their pain, their confusion, their hope, the media misrepresentation, and the world's disdain of the Jewish people and the nation of Israel even and perhaps more so today, when Israel appears to be coming under greater criticism for raking those very steps of self-defense which we in America take for granted as our sovereign moral right to take in defense of ourselves and our interests.

As a believer, I have and can have no doubt that mankind must learn that obedience towards G-d and His commandments is the key to progress, whether personal or corporate, national or international. Disobedience, on the other hand, can lead only to great difficulty. This too is the story of the Jewish people and the nation of Israel. And, indeed it appears that G-d's chosen people have ascended to heights and descended to depths far beyond our experience - in both blessings and curses - in progress and disaster.

In considering the history of Israel, however, this principle alone is insufficient to explain the great magnitude of Israel's sufferings. There is another dimension. Through the centuries, the millennia, Israel has been and continues to be a tangible and visible target for dark spiritual forces which are directed against the living G-d himself. No one can touch G-d; but the individual Jew and the nation of Israel are within reach of those whose hatred is directed against G-d, and who would foil the fulfillment of His purposes and disrupt His plan for the people of His covenant and the nation of Israel.

This hatred has been manifested time and again throughout the ages. To name only a sampling, there have been the crusades, the inquisition, the pogroms. In this century, we have seen the Holocaust, as well as the humiliation of and later reneging on, numerous agreements regarding the land of promise. Since the re-establishment of the State of Israel in 1948, there have been many wars and many more terrorist attacks. Most recently, there has been the Gulf War with scud missiles, threatening chemical mayhem. Then there was, and continues to be, the forced pressure of the 'peace' negotiations and calls of "land for peace" despite the fact that Israel is the only nation on Earth that was created by a sovereign act of G-d (Genesis 15) and whose borders are defined by G-d (Numbers 34:1-12). For in (Exodus 32: 13) He said, "...All of this land which I have spoken of will I give to your descendants and they shall inherit it **forever**."

And when in the summer of the year 2000, the Prime Minister of Israel indicated that in return for the much prayed for peace Israel would be willing to give most all of the territory of the Holy Land reconquered in the 1967 War - a war commenced by the Arabs with the declared purpose of destroying Israel - to the Palestinians for them to be a state, those very

Palestinians rejected the offer, declaring that the Jews had no right to Jerusalem or to the Temple Mount, that the Bible was "forged" to show such a connection between the people of Israel and the site of His House, and then commenced a wave of terrorism, sending human bombs to kill and maim teenagers at discotheques and families at pizza lunches.

Yet the recent events in the land of Israel notwithstanding, with sorrow and regret, we must admit the truth and confess that the greatest sufferings imposed on the Jewish people and Israel throughout history have come from the so-called Christian church and from those confessing the Christian faith. <u>For this we must all ask their forgiveness</u>. The forces directed against the Jews have misrepresented G-d and have wrongly interpreted His Word in an attempt to rob Israel of its inheritance which is based on (Genesis 17:7-8) a sovereign promise from G-d (Exodus 6:4) and an everlasting covenant (Deuteronomy 4:31). Despite the fact that these expressions of evil are totally contrary to G-d's everlasting covenant, His unchanging nature and purpose, these actions were and continue to be "justified" by these evil men and nations for their own ends.

But as the Bible declares, G-d HAS NOT forsaken His covenant people (Jeremiah 31:31-40); and, "as new covenant believers, we are commanded by G-d in the Bible to stand together with the Jewish people whom the world has abused, As the fulfillment of prophecy is for the Jewish people - for them the realization of their covenant and for them the answer to their prayers of countless generations:

"And I will plant them upon their land, and they shall no more be pulled up out of their land which I have given them, saith the Lord thy God." (Amos 9:14-15).

John Brown

Founder (Amos 3:7)

THE SCRIPTURES GIVEN TO JOHN BROWN

THE QUESTION AND THE ANSWER...The Blessings of the Fathers (*Genesis Chapters 17, 27, 49 and Deuteronomy Chapters 32,33*)

The economic and political stability of Israel, indeed, its very survival is at stake not in any small measure because of its dependence on imported oil and gas. The desire to free Israel of such dependence has opened up unexplored areas of Israel and, today, more sophisticated exploitation and drilling techniques than previously used are being utilized to assess the oil potential of those areas.

The State of Israel lies in the heart of the Middle East and is surrounded by areas in neighboring Arab countries which contain the world's largest oil fields. These oil fields are the blessings and posterity which G-d had promised Abraham also for his son Ishmael in (Genesis 17:18-20) and by Isaac's blessing also of his son Esau in (Genesis 27:38-39). The genealogies of Ishmael (Genesis 25:12-18) and Esau (Genesis 36) show that their descendants became the inhabitants of modern day Saudi Arabia -and other Arab countries from Egypt to Iraq, Jordan to Yemen.

The State of Israel, as a member of the free world and as the only true, stable democracy in the Middle East, strives to find oil to remain independent from outside political pressures.

In 1988, the Government of Israel, acting through the government-owned Oil Exploration Investments Ltd., its affiliates and subsidiaries and geological consultants of renowned international reputation, established the hydrocarbon potential of Israel, and validated the existence of significant quantities of recoverable oil and gas in the Land of Israel, as also exist in the neighboring countries of the Middle East.

Past exploration efforts have yielded several small on-shore discoveries and the recent, significant gas fields off-shore in the Mediterranean Sea. But the "real potential" still awaits discovery!

Following continued assessment of all geological and geophysical data, renowned petroleum engineers, geologists and geophysicists continue to ask ... "where is the most logical place to drill where we can be sure of 'tapping' those vast reservoirs of oil?"

Yet, there is an "ANSWER", and **it** is found in the most "overlooked" source of geological information available to mankind today the Bible! The archaeologists have found the Bible to be their unerring guide to hidden treasures ... Why cannot the geologists utilize the same "tool" to find this oil?

So we searched the Bible and found numerous occasions where, I believe, the Bible in describing the division of the Land of Israel among the sons of Jacob - commencing in Genesis (Chapter 49) when Jacob on his deathbed summons his sons and says *"Gather yourselves together, that I might tell you that which shall befall you in the LAST DAYS"* (Genesis 49:1) and concluding in Deuteronomy (Chapters 32 and 33) with Moses' song of praise of G-d and his blessings of the twelve tribes as G-d prepares him to view the "Promised Land" which HE had given to HIS chosen "Children of Israel" - makes direct reference to the existence of OIL in Israel.

So, friends of Israel, as we begin "The Great Treasure Hunt" ... may we join hands with the Government of Israel and its people and together look toward and pray for "the discovery of OIL in their homeland, the Land of Israel" and on the "Head of Joseph" as promised in the Torah by the G-d of Abraham, Isaac and Jacob (Genesis 49:25, 26) (Deuteronomy 33:13-16); and then G-d said, *"I will even gather you from the peoples, and assemble you out of the countries where ye have been scattered, and I will give you the land of Israel"* (Ezekiel 11:17) and Israel will be graciously comforted and restored. (Micah 7:18-20), (Ezekiel 37:15-28)

THE VISION ... The Oil of Is'ra-el

While visiting Israel with Alger Wolfe in May 1983, John Brown's prayer to the G-d of Abraham, Isaac and Jacob was for oil to be found in Israel. This prayer and G-d's specific instruction to John were based on the Biblical portion describing the Dedication of the First Temple in Jerusalem and Solomon's prayers thereat. (I Kings 8:22-66)

ONE ... The Prayer

"Moreover concerning a stranger [John Brown], *that is not of thy people Israel but cometh out of a far country* [U.S.A.] *for thy name's sake: (for they shall hear of thy great name, and of thy strong hand and of thy stretched out arm); when he shall come and pray towards this house; hear thou in heaven thy dwelling place, and do according to ALL that the stranger calleth to thee for* [Oil for Israel]: *that all the people of the earth may know thy name, to fear thee, as do thy people Israel and that thy may know that this house, which I have builded, is called by thy name. '(1 Kings 8:41-43).*

TWO ... The Instructions

"And it shall come to pass, if ye shall hearken diligently unto my commandments which I command you this day, to love the Lord your God and to serve Him with all your heart and with all your soul, that I will give you the rain of your land in his due season, the early rain and the late rain, that thou mayest gather in thy corn, and thy wine, and thine OIL [the OIL of Israel]." *(Deuteronomy 11:13-14)*

THREE ... The Evidence

"Then thou shalt see, and flow together, and thine heart shall fear, and be enlarged- because the abundance of the sea shall

be converted unto thee, the forces of the Gentiles shall come unto thee." (Isaiah 60:5)

These three specific sets of instructions received by John Brown in 1983 from G-d while in the land of Israel, were a consuming "fire" which has been born by him through the years for the exact purpose that G-d first lit it in his heart! Today, G-d continues to confirm, by HIS Word, the reality of HIS promise when HE also promised...

"For surely there is an end and thy expectation shall not be cut off" (Proverbs 23:18)

THE CALLING... Tell Them...

So, then He told me to *"write the vision"* (Habakkuk 2:2, 3) and tell them:

"And the word of the Lord came unto me, saying, 'Son of man, what is that proverb that ye have in the land of Israel, saying, The days are prolonged, and every vision faileth? Tell them therefore, Thus saith the Lord God; I will make this proverb to cease, and they shall no more use it as a proverb in Israel but say unto them, The days are at hand, and the effect of every vision. For there shall be no more any vain vision nor flattering divination within the house of Israel. For I am the Lord: I will speak, and the word that I shall speak shall come to pass; it shall be no more prolonged: for in your days, 0 rebellious house, will l say the word, and will perform it, saith the Lord God"

"Again the word of the Lord came to me saying, 'Son of man, behold they of the house of Israel say, The vision that he seeth is for many days to come, and he prophesieth of the times that are far off. Therefore say unto them, Thus saith the Lord God; There shall none of my words be prolonged any more, but the word which I have spoken shall be done, saith the Lord God'"
(Ezekiel 12: 21-28)

THE PROMISES...Also Unto the Gentiles *(Leviticus 19:33, 34)*

For the prophets foretold that Gentiles (Isaiah 55:5) would also call upon G-d and they too would serve him (Zephaniah 3:9) and he would answer their prayers (Isaiah 65:24) and he would save them (Isaiah 52:10) and set them in the land! (Isaiah 14:1) For it is also written:

"Also the sons of the stranger, that join themselves to the Lord, to serve Him, and to love the name of the Lord, to be His servants, every one that keepeth the Sabbath and does not profane it, and all that hold fast to my covenant. Even them will I bring to my holy mountain, and make them joyful in my house of prayer; their burnt offerings and their sacrifices shall be accepted on my altar: for my house shall be called a house of prayer for all peoples.' (Isaiah 56: 6-7)

A NEW COVENANT PEOPLE ... *Jeremiah 31: 31-34)*

For G-d has promised that not only would He honor his First Covenant and would cause the Jews to return (Jeremiah 33:14-26), but that one day He would also make a New Covenant (Jeremiah 31:33-34) and (in Hosea 2:23) He said: *"...And I will say to them that were not my people; Thou art my people!"* And they shall say, *"you are my God"* and they will help restore the Nation of Israel and many people would come to the Land of Israel to seek the G-d of Israel (Zechariah 8:20-23) (Isaiah 65:1) and these strangers who dwelt among the people of Israel would also share in the promised inheritance (Ezekiel 47:21-23) and... *"the stranger that dwells with you shall be to you as one born among you."* (Leviticus 19:34) For G-d's promise to Abraham was, *"and in thy seed shall **all the nations of the earth be blessed.**"* (Genesis 22:18)

So now we, a new covenant people, (Deuteronomy 29:12-15) have come to the land of Israel to claim our promised inheritance and to receive the blessings of Abraham (Galatians 3:6-14). For it is also written, *"...is He the God of the Jews only? Is HE not the God of the Gentiles? Yes, of the Gentiles also"* (Romans 3:29-30) for G-d hath not cast away HIS people which HE foreknew. *"For if their* [the Jewish people] *being cast away is the reconciling of the world, what will their acceptance be but life from the dead?"* (Romans 11:1-24). Because, *"that blindness in part has happened to Israel until the fullness of the Gentiles be come in. And so all Israel will be saved."* (Romans 11:24-36) Therefore:

As a Christian, one must recognize that it is written *"... if* [we] *the Gentiles have been made partakers of their* [Israel's] *spiritual things, their* [Gentiles'] *duty is also to minister to them* [Israel] *in material things."* (Romans 15:27) Because *"the G-d of heaven He will prosper us* [Zion]" (Nehemiah 2:20) with the oil of Israel ... so that we a new covenant people of Zion will minister and assist "Israel in their petroleum and material needs." Because, as touching the election, *"they* [the Jewish People] *are beloved for the sake of the fathers."* (Romans 11:28) And, when they do turn to the Lord, the veil on their hearts will be taken away. (2 Corinthians 3:14-16)

THE PURPOSE...

To Receive The Blessings Of Jacob *(Genesis 49:1-2 and 22-26)*

Zion Oil & Gas was ordained by G-d for the express purpose of discovering oil and gas in the Land of Israel and to bless the Jewish people and the nation of Israel and the body of Christ. (Isaiah 23:18) I believe that G-d has promised in the Bible to bless Israel with one of the world's largest oil and gas fields and this will be discovered in the last days before the Messiah returns and that it will be found on the Ma'anit License and the Joseph Permit, both being on the Head of Joseph (Genesis 49:1-2 and 22-26):

"And Jacob called unto his Sons, and said, Gather yourselves together, that I may tell you that which shall befall you in the last days. Gather yourselves together, and hear, ye sons of Jacob; and listen unto Israel your Father ... Joseph is a fruitful bough, a fruitful bough by a well; whose branches run over the wall. The archers fiercely attacked him and shot at him and hated him; but his bow abode in strength, and the arms of his hands were made supple by the hands of the mighty God of Jacob (by the name of shepherd, the Rock of Israel), by the God of thy father who shall help thee; and by the Almighty who shall bless thee, with blessings of the heaven above, blessings of the deep [the Oil of Israel] *that couches beneath; blessings of the breasts and the womb. The blessings of thy Father are mighty beyond the blessings of the eternal mountains, the blessings of the everlasting hills* [Oil]*, they shall be on the head of Joseph, and on the crown of the head of him that was separated from his brothers."*

...And The Blessing Of Moses *(Deuteronomy 33:1,13-19)*

"And this is the blessing which Moses the man of GOD blessed the sons of Israel before his death." (Deuteronomy 33:1)

"...And of Joseph he said, blessed of the Lord be his land, for the precious things of heaven, for the dew and for the deep [the Oil of Israel] *that coucheth beneath, and for the precious fruits brought forth by the sun, and for the precious things put forth by the moon, and for the chief things of the ancient mountains and for the precious things of primordial hills* [Oil] *and fullness thereof and for the Good will of HIM that dwelt in the bush; let the blessing* [the Oil of Israel] *come upon the head of Joseph, and upon the top of the head of him that was separated from his brethren;" (Deuteronomy 33:13-16);*

"They shall call the peoples to the mountain; there they shall offer sacrifices of righteousness; for they shall suck of the abundance of the seas, and of treasures [the Oil of Israel] *hid in the sand "(Deuteronomy 33:19,)*

THE JOSEPH PROJECT

...The Inheritance *(Genesis 48:1 5-22)*

"Joseph shall have two portions. And you shall inherit it, one as well as another; that concerning which I lifted up my hand to give it to your fathers; and this land shall fall to you as an inheritance." (Ezekiel 47:13-14)

"And it shall come to pass, that you shall divide it by lot for an inheritance to you, and to the strangers [Gentile believers] *that sojourn among you, who shall beget children among you: and they shall be to you as those born in the country among the children of Israel; they shall have an inheritance with you among the tribes of Israel. And it shall come to pass, that in whatever tribe the stranger may stay there you shall give him his inheritance, says the Lord GOD." (Ezekiel 4 7:22-23)*

...The Plan ...By Faith *(Hebrews 11:1-40)*

Zion's approach is somewhat unprecedented ...and that is because of its founder's, John Brown's, FAITH in G-d and HIS promises (Joshua 1:8) and in G-d's faithfulness and ability to perform all HIS Word, as we also walk in the steps of faith as Our Father Abraham walked. (Romans 4:11-25) And Jesus said, *"It is written* [Deuteronomy 8:3], *Man shall not live by bread alone, but by every word of God."* (Luke 4:4)

Now, *"FAITH is the substance of things* [the Oil of Israel] *hoped for, the evidence of things not seen....* [And, it is also written that] *By FAITH Abraham, when he was tested, offered up Isaac, and.. By FAITH Isaac blessed Jacob and Esau concerning things to come; ...By FAITH Jacob, when he was dying, blessed each of the sons of Joseph."* (Hebrews 11:1-22) G-d's word establishes and so states "... *The JUST shall live by his FAITH* (Habakkuk 2:4) ...*But without FAITH, it is impossible to please HIM.* "(Hebrews 10:38 and 11:6)

For: We worship by faith as Abel. We walk by faith as Enoch. We work by faith as Noah. We live by faith as Abraham. We govern by faith as Moses. We follow by faith as Israel. We fight by faith as Joshua. We conquer by faith as Gideon. By faith we are patient in suffering, courageous in battle, made strong out of weakness, and are victorious in defeat. We are more than conquerors by our faith seeing *"...there is one God who will justify the circumcised By Faith and the uncircumcised through faith.* "(Romans 3:29-30) So, it is only through faith in JESUS CHRIST that we are saved. *"It is written in the prophets, 'And they shall all be taught by God'* (Isaiah 54:13) *Therefore everyone who hath heard, AND HATH LEARNED OF THE FATHER, cometh unto me."* *(John 6:45-51)*

From its inception, G-d's plan was born through Faith in G-d's Word into the heart of John Brown, Zion's founder, and, in all matters concerning Zion, the Word of G-d has been the basis of John Brown's conduct and actions: For it is written, *"This book of Law shall not depart from your mouth, but you shall meditate in it day and night, that you may observe to do according to all that is written in it."* (Joshua 1:8) Consequently, the founder of *Zion* shall respect *and "Fear God, and keep HIS commandments: for that is the WHOLE duty of man."* (Ecclesiastes 12:13)

NOW BY FAITH ... The Ma'anit/Joseph License #298

As of May, 2005 drilling is nearing completion at Ma'anit #1 well in ISRAEL. For I believe that G-d has promised in the Bible that, in the last days, oil will be discovered in Israel on the head of Joseph. (Genesis 49:1)

... *"by the God of thy father who shall help thee; and by the ALMIGHTY who shall bless thee, with blessings of HEAVEN above, blessings of the DEEP* [**the Oil of Israel**] *THAT LIETH BENEATH; ... they shall be on the head of Joseph, and on the crown of him that was separated from his brethren."*

(Genesis 49:25-26)

... "And of Joseph he said, blessed of the LORD be his land, for the precious things of HEAVEN, for the dew and for the DEEP [the Oil of Israel] *THAT COUCHETH BENEATH ... and, for the chief thing of the ancient mountains and for the precious things* [Meged] *of the primordial hills* [Oil] *and fullness thereof, and for the Good will of **Him** that dwelt in the bush; **let the blessing** [the Oil of Israel] come upon the head of Joseph, and upon the top of the head of him that was separated from his brethren".* (Deuteronomy 33:13-16) *"And of Asher he said, Be Asher blessed above sons; let him be acceptable to his brethren, and let him DIP HIS FOOT IN OIL."* (Deuteronomy 33:24)

(See biblical map on the next page for the location of the Ma'anit/Joseph License, and Ma'anit #1 well in relation to the lands of Joseph's children, Ephraim and Manasseh and the land of Asher.)

NOTICE:

The Twelve Tribes in Canaan

The Foot of Asher to be dipped in oil on the Head of Joseph.

Deuteronomy 33:24 -

And of Asher he said, "Let Asher be blessed with children; let him be acceptable to his brethren, and let him dip his foot in oil".

Other books by James R. Spillman

➤ Omega Cometh
➤ Animal Church
➤ A Conspiracy of Angels
➤ The Fire of God
➤ The Resurrection Clock
➤ The Great Treasure Hunt
➤ Treasures of the Deep

Visit: *www.JimSpillmanMinistries.org* for a full listing of resources available from the works of James R. Spillman

About the Authors

James R. Spillman, author, evangelist, and Christian educator was widely known for his charismatic ministry and personality. An ordained Conservative Baptist minister since 1960, Jim served in many churches of varied denominations and backgrounds. As an evangelist and author Jim used his unique mix of spiritual and educational depth with humor to reach people where they were. Audiences around the world were captivated by the power of God demonstrated in his life and brought to Christ for salvation, baptism, healing, and other mighty works of renewal.

Jim left this earth for his eternal home in late 2002. His work, however, continues to touch people's lives through books, and recorded material that remain as fresh and relevant today as when they were first produced. Jim's story and resources can be found at ***www.JimSpillmanMinistries.org***.

Steven M. Spillman, one of six children of Jim and Nancy Spillman, is the founder and president of True Potential Publishing, Inc. True Potential Publishing's full resource offering can be found at ***www.tppress.com***.

Steve is the creator of the ***www.OilinIsrael.net*** website and editor of the *Purpose Weekly* newsletter. For a free subscription to *Purpose Weekly*, visit ***www.gotpotential.org*** or send an e-mail to ***truepotential@tppress.com***.

Additional copies of ***Breaking the Treasure Code, The Hunt for Israel's Oil*** can be purchased through your local bookstore or by visiting www.tppress.com.

Telephone orders can be placed at (864) 836-4111

Fax orders can be placed at (864) 610-8047

Postal orders can be placed by writing to:

True Potential Publishing

PO Box 904, Travelers Rest, SC 29690

Please include a check or money order for $14.95 per copy plus $5.00 per order (not per copy) for shipping. South Carolina residents please add 6% sales tax.

Attention churches and study groups: For quantity discounts please contact the publisher:

Telephone: (864) 836-4111   Fax: (864) 610-8047

E-mail: info@tppress.com